WEIGHT WATCHERS
COOK BOOK

WEIGHT WATCHERS COOK BOOK

by Jean Nidetch

Drawings by Ivy Bottini

Hearthside Press, Incorporated
Publishers   •   New York

CONTENTS

ACKNOWLEDGEMENTS

First, I wish to express appreciation to Nedda C. Anders, editor and co-publisher of Hearthside Press, Inc. Her involvement was far more than a routine editorial one and without her this book could not have been written.

Second, I would like to acknowledge my indebtedness to the physicians, nutritionists, public health workers and home economists who have specialized in the field of obesity.

Finally, I would like to express my gratitude to those whose belief in me started it all—my husband, my sons, David and Richard, and my associates at Weight Watchers, especially Felice Lippert. Also to the members, graduates and instructors, to our loyal staff, and to the people who conduct authorized classes following our program and under our franchise. For space reasons, I can say thank you to them only collectively, but I could fill many pages with individual names. This book is as much their work as it is mine.

INTRODUCTION TO WEIGHT WATCHERS

All my life, until 1961, I suffered from obesity. A fat little girl, a chubby teenager, I was matronly at twenty and obese by thirty. Of course, in those days I would never describe myself in those words. Then I was "big-boned," "large-framed," "glandular," or a victim of "hereditary overweight." But I really did not believe my own excuses and kept trying desperately to reduce. For the major part of my life I alternately starved my body or overindulged it. Although I lost weight dozens of times, it always came back. With the poundage came depression, frustration and the torment of knowing that once again I was a failure.

Nevertheless, I did not give up my dream of having a slim figure, with the youthfulness, vigor and personal happiness which it promised. Therefore, in 1961 I registered for an obesity clinic at the New York City Board of Health. Here I acquired some first-hand experience with a *good* reducing menu, one which I was to follow for 10 weeks. Although I am not a nutritionist, it was plain to me that theirs was not a "crash" diet, but a conservative plan for eating of the kind invariably recommended or approved by nutritionists and dieticians. It was low in fat, sugar and starch but contained all the elements of good nutrition. So I stayed on the diet losing weight sensibly but steadily. Years later, still a size 12, I am convinced that only a slow, consistent program of weight reduction can be successful in the long run.

But to get back to that 10-week period. The weight I had lost made only a dent in my bulk but it was an observable dent, and friends began to ask questions. Although I did not know it at the time, in answering these questions and in passing along my enthusiasm for a sensible eating pattern—as a contrast to the faddist glamour diets which obese people often go on—I was laying the groundwork for Weight Watchers Inc. The fact is that our organization is based on the principles of good menu planning, and on having ex-fatties who have won the war against obesity point out the problems, pitfalls and pleasures which pave the road to a trim figure.

Anyway, as I answered the questions which interested friends kept asking, the desire to pass along the nutritional knowledge I had acquired became more and more insistent. Consequently, when six obese friends wanted diet details, I invited them to meet at my house, where I could tell what I knew and where we could talk over common problems related to overeating. We helped ourselves in varied ways. We discussed the reasons for our overeating, the excuses we gave ourselves, even the places where we hid sweets and cookies to keep our families from finding them. Believe me, it helped to know that I was not the only person in the world who hid chocolate cakes in laundry hampers!

Soon the little group of six grew to thirty as friends, relatives, acquaintances begged to join. The group grew too big for my house, so we rented a basement. Then I was asked to talk to groups in other areas. I went gladly, for I had begun to feel that even if my life served no other purpose I could help people understand and conquer their obesity. In the spring of 1963 we finally rented our first large meeting hall, in Little Neck, New York, and Weight Watchers became a corporation. Today, there are more than 200 branches all over America, and soon there will be branches overseas as well. Hardly a week passes that someone does not write us asking for a franchise to give a Weight Watchers class in their city.

There are statistics to the effect that 79,000,000 adult Americans are overweight and about 9,500,000 of them are dieting at any one time. I am no longer surprised by these figures. But it is apparent from our mail that overweight is by no means only an American problem. Letters come from England, France, Israel and even from as far away as New Zealand. So many people who have successfully fought this battle of obesity under our guidance had told their friends and families all over the world about us, that a tremendous influx of mail resulted. The story of Weight Watchers was even printed in a French newspaper.

This tremendous response to the Weight Watchers program is very significant. All of you who have been overweight for any length of time know that diets are always with us. Some highly-rated ones slip into oblivion as nutritionists and physicians find and expose their weaknesses. Other diets fall from grace because they bring only temporary weight loss and massive disenchantment results when the weight comes back. It is true that although we are no doubt the largest organization of its kind in the world we cannot quote percentages. Someday, God willing, we will undertake such a study.

Meanwhile, however, we have other evidence to go on, for at our meetings, when new members are asked why they joined us, we hear over and over again something like: "Because this is the only diet my sister (or mother, neighbor, friend or cousin) ever stayed slim on." So our tremendous following is, we know, the result of word-of-mouth recommendation. This is our proof that the W.W.* Program has been an overwhelming success.

What does all this mean to you? It means that you can take part in a program that has been tested and proven for years. It means you can create a new image for yourself. Literally it means a new life for you no matter what your past case history.

Before you join the Weight Watchers through the pages of this book, I ask first that you get your doctor's approval. Then I ask that you commit yourself confidently to our program. Losing weight is not a simple chore but Weight Watchers have discovered that *it can be done*—safely, sanely, and lastingly.

THE FOOD—From the very beginning, when we were a group of six having our first meeting, it was only natural that food should be a big subject for us. It was important to discuss methods of preparing the allowed or, as we called it, legal foods. Questions would arise about the menu, interpretations might be necessary. Of course we exchanged recipes. One day someone brought in a recipe for a tasty apple, baked to a lovely red with a non-caloric carbonated drink used as a baste and cinnamon for seasoning. Another time, a member gave us a recipe using the "skim milk" which is required on our plan for good nutrition—and a satisfying rich malted was added to our cuisine. Then there was a delicious French toast, made without butter. This was created by the wife of a member who for twenty years had eaten nothing else for breakfast! And so it continued. Imaginative cooks kept bringing in their good ideas for dishes that others could share with them. With such a wealth to choose from, no one felt deprived, no one went hungry. And so, the recipe exchange which began in our early days has led directly to this cookbook.

OVEREATING IS A HABIT—Many books have been written about how to train oneself to new habits, and it is a field in itself. And, as I

* Abbreviation for Weight Watchers.

already told you, I am not a physician, not a psychologist, not a nutritionist, but I know that overeating is a habit which can be conquered like any other habit. All you need is the will to do so and enough drive to get you started.

Perhaps you make the same excuses for overweight that I did—glands, metabolism, heredity. In most cases, these are just excuses, not facts.

(However, if you have any physical ailment requiring the attention of a doctor, or if you have any reservation about applying the principles of this program to yourself, by all means submit this diet to your physician before you begin. His approval may be just the confidence you need to make a good start. Also, I would like to mention that at Weight Watchers, we always ask pregnant women to bring an obstetrician's consent and I wish you could see some of the many notes of commendation which come back to us!)

So unless your physician has told you otherwise, realize that you are fat because you overeat, and you overeat not from hunger, but from habit. Therefore, follow the menu without any deviation whatever. Tell yourself that first you will get through one meal. Do so. Proceed one meal at a time, one day at a time, one week at a time. Taking one step at a time, strengthening yourself slowly, you cannot fail.

The next time you begin to bite into a candy bar, order a fattening dessert from a restaurant menu, walk into the bakery for a Danish pastry, stop for a minute. Ask yourself: "Would I rather have this or a slim young figure?" In most cases, even that one-minute stop will convince you you have everything to gain by beginning to lose.

NO CRASH DIETING PLEASE—Because you must learn new habits of eating, it is useless for you to go on "crash" or "fad" diets, or to take diet pills or appetite depressants of any kind. Why learn to use a crutch when you can learn how to walk properly? Another point, don't surround yourself with temptation by buying cookies and candies. Even a four-year-old can understand if told that mommy needs his help because she wants to become his "beautiful mommy."

THE GAMES PEOPLE PLAY—I mentioned earlier that our original Weight Watchers discussed common problems and excuses for overeating. Over the years, we have heard every kind of excuse. Now, when I train our instructors (every one of them must go through a rigorous training program after his or her weight reduction) I warn them to beware of the excuses which members will bring into class by the bagful, to explain why they did not lose weight, why they cheated, etc. Throughout these pages you will find cartoon drawings to illustrate some of the favorite rationalizations we hear.

WHY WE DON'T COUNT CALORIES—In the early days of our Weight Watchers classes, someone was always striking a little bargain with himself and with us, cheating in small ways. "I had a piece of chocolate cake, but I really saved 200 calories because I skipped lunch," or "We were entertaining my husband's clients and a drink only has 100 calories so I thought I could skip breakfast next morning to make up for it." (You will find some advice about handling this cocktail-party problem in the menu section—see index for page number.)

Of course, you cannot break bad eating habits, or make good new ones, by this kind of petty larceny, so we are firm about this rule:

> *No alcohol*
> *No skipping meals*
> *No counting calories*

WEIGHT WATCHERS ON THE GO—In the years in which we have been conducting Weight Watchers Programs, many working people, traveling salesmen, active club women, lecturers, physicians, hostesses who prided themselves on their cooking ability, and many, many teenagers having lunch in school cafeterias have been enrolled in our groups, have lost weight, and have maintained their weight loss. Therefore I know, our instructors know, *and you know* that you can stick to your menu no matter what your home, social, business, or school life may be. On page 22 we give some easy menus for people who eat away from home.

HOW LONG DOES IT TAKE TO LOSE WEIGHT?—Since the whole program is based on changing your eating habits, not on an easy-come, easy-go weight loss, we do not encourage you to skip meals, or to eat less than is permitted. On the contrary, we insist that you follow our program to the letter, no matter how much weight you have to lose and how eager you are to lose it quickly. The heavier you are, the bigger the loss of weight at the beginning, but in general we prefer that you do not feel you are competing with anyone. The amount of weight you lose is dependent on many factors which vary from one individual to another (but you can be sure that your body will respond to the highly nutritious food you are now encouraged to eat). The important thing to remember is that you must survive each day (one day at a time) without deviating from the set pattern of three *complete* meals. With this method, it is inevitable that you should eventually show a weight loss and at the same time feel well and able to cope with the next day.

Many of our members attend classes once a week for 16 weeks, in order to earn the W.W. award—a pin for women and a tie bar for men. If they have reached their ideal weight at the end of this period, they may go on "Maintenance," attending classes once a month for as long as they feel the need for inspiration and encouragement. If, after 16 weeks, they have not yet reached "goal," members continue to come once a week until they too are ready for Maintenance.

MAINTENANCE PROGRAM—In giving you our plan through this book, we make the same recommendation to you as we do to members, that is, adhere to it for a minimum of sixteen weeks so that you not only take off weight, but recondition yourself to control your eating habits.

If you have reached your weight goal before the 16 weeks are over, continue to follow our basic menu, which has all the elements you need for good nutrition. However, you can add to it foods that you like, or use larger quantities of the recommended foods. Check your weight at least once a week to be sure it stays put.

DOES WRINKLING FOLLOW WEIGHT LOSS?—One of the most remarkable qualities about our W.W. Program is that we have never seen it accompanied by loss of skin tone. I believe that by losing weight slowly, and eating properly, you give your skin more time to shrink. From our experience with so many members, we have seen people lose well over 100 pounds without any noticeable sign that they have ever been overweight. It is always a joy to us to meet a member who weighed in at over 250 pounds after the loss of 100 or more pounds. What a strikingly healthy, firm-toned, happy-looking individual has been hidden under the flabbiness! So if you have postponed getting started for reasons of vanity, believe me, your skin won't sag, you won't wrinkle, you won't look older, and you won't have less energy. Just the reverse will happen, and if you are in normal health, you should feel better and look far better than you ever did.

The walls of our meeting places are lined with before-and-after pictures of members, and if you ever attend one of our programs you can see for yourself how much more attractive they become after losing weight.

WHAT GOES ON AT OUR MEETINGS?—There is a great deal of curiosity about our meetings. At a typical meeting, each member is weighed in private. The weight loss is then recorded on a card, and the instructor discusses the member's achievement as evidenced by the card. Often, successful weight losers are eager to tell their own reducing stories and are encouraged to do so. Listening to them can be very helpful to new members. Frequently, too, veteran members are present to be seen "in the flesh" and compared with their "before" pictures which are also displayed. Another source of strength is the instructor. All of our instructors have suffered from a weight problem and, by our requirements, have lost weight under the Weight Watchers Program. She or he (we have many male instructors) stands before the audience—slim, confident, attractive, and most important, full of compassion and empathy for those who are struggling with mankind's biggest enemy. (Yes, overweight is undesirable not only for cosmetic reasons, but it is considered a cause of heart disease.)

Only registered members may attend meetings and no one with less than 10 pounds to lose is accepted as a member. This policy was instituted primarily to protect overweight Weight Watchers from those who would like to attend simply to kill time or to satisfy curiosity.

NOW LET'S TALK ABOUT YOU—Chances are you are a professional weight loser. You have probably lost weight a thousand times, and gained it back just as often. Now once again you are planning to go on a diet.

What started this? Maybe you're tired of having a fat husband and a fat dog. Maybe you ran out of friends fatter than you are. Maybe you're bored with being "so jolly" and want to give your mouth muscles a chance to relax. Or maybe you're tired of having people say, "With a face like yours how did you ever let yourself go?"

Whatever the reason please don't start this W.W. program unless you're desperate. Deep-down desperate. So desperate that you are miserable. So desperate that you are in dead earnest. And when and if you reach that point, we can help you. We have helped tougher cases.

One such case came to our office in Forest Hills ten months ago. He was 20 years old and weighed 429 pounds, but there was nothing physically wrong with him. This boy came up to me and said, "Mrs. Nidetch, I can't remember ever wearing a bathing suit. Can you help me?"

Yes, we helped him, or let us say, he helped himself! So far George has lost 78 pounds and is still going down. By summer, I think he will have his wish. And he won't stop until his weight reaches a normal range. He knows it and I know it.

Most of the people who come to us are not this obese, but where do you think 429 pounds starts? It starts with 10 pounds, then 20, then 50. It goes off the same way, a few pounds at a time, one day at a time, one hour at a time. So when you start this program, remember, it will require your desperation, your sincerity, your co-operation and your patience.

And now that I have told you about myself, about the program which has helped so many thousands of men, women, and children, and what it requires of you, I would like to introduce you to the actual menus and recipes.

Jean Nidetch, Founder and Director

Spring 1966

RULES AND MENU PLANS FOR ALL

Rules for All Weight Watchers

1. Eat only the foods listed in your Menu Plan, in the quantities specified and at the meals specified. Weigh your portions until you can judge them accurately. Watch your count and list on Daily Food Record (page 280) any limited foods which are included in a recipe you are using.

2. EGGS. Limit them to 4-7 per week. They may be taken only at breakfast or luncheon, not at dinner.

3. CHEESE. Only hard cheese or pot, cottage or farmer cheese is allowed, and only at breakfast or luncheon (legal cheeses by name are given on page 40). Follow your Menu Plan for the amounts you are permitted.

4. FISH. You must eat a minimum of five Group A fish meals each week, luncheons or dinners. You may have fish more often if you wish, at breakfast, luncheon or dinner. Group A fish are listed on page 56. Do not add fat when cooking fish. Do not use smoked fish. Add 2 ounces to raw fish weight to allow for loss in cooking and also 2 ounces for fish with bones.

5. MEAT AND POULTRY. Provided you use the specified number of fish meals, some of your luncheons and dinners may be selected from Group A meats and poultry or Group B fish. See pages 56 and 96 for lists. You may select Group B meats and poultry for no more than 3 meals a week. Add 2 ounces to raw meat weight to allow for loss in cooking and also 2 ounces for meat with bones.

6. LIMITED VEGETABLES (see list on page 183) must be eaten one a day, at dinner only, 1 portion only. Vary your selection from day to day. One serving is 4 ounces, or ½ cup, or 1 medium-sized unit. For example: 1 medium artichoke, 1 medium tomato or ½ cup diced tomato, ½ cup shelled peas, etc.

7. UNLIMITED VEGETABLES are listed on page 144. They may be taken at any time, before, during or after meals.

8. Condiments and seasonings such as bouillon, herbs, and spices, salt, pepper, and paprika, vinegar and wine vinegar, tea, coffee, horseradish, soy sauce, lemons, limes, etc., are unlimited. See Chapter 8 for sauces, dressings and dips which may be used at any time and in any amount, except for those containing ingredients marked with an asterisk. A few drops of vanilla flavoring and similar extracts·may be used to flavor permitted foods. Page 275 has an expanded list of unlimited seasonings.

9. FRUIT. See your Menu Plan for the amount of fruit you are allowed. One daily fruit must be either orange or grapefruit (high in Vitamin C). One half-cup or the following amounts count as 1 fruit:

1 medium apple	2-inch wedge honeydew melon
½ cantaloupe	1 orange
½ grapefruit	¼ medium-sized fresh pineapple

No bananas, cherries, watermelon, dried fruits, grapes.

10. MILK. Powdered skim milk, buttermilk, or evaporated skim milk must be included in your daily program, according to the amount given in your Menu Plan. You may use milk at any time you wish, with meals or as a snack, but only in the specified amount. Milk used in coffee or tea, or in any of the recipes, must be counted (see page 280 for Food Record).

11. BREAD. Eat enriched or whole grain packaged bread according to the amount allowed in your Menu Plan.

    No rolls, bagels, biscuits, muffins, crackers, cereals, or special breads.

12. Do *not* eat or drink the following, except for legal recipes given in this book.

alcoholic beverages, including beer, wine, whiskey	jello
	jelly
	ketchup
avocado	mayonnaise
bacon or back fat	muffins
bagels	nuts
biscuits	oil
butter	olives
cake	pancakes
candy	peanut butter
cereals	pies
coconut	popcorn
cookies	potato chips
crackers	pretzels
cream cheese	puddings
doughnuts	rolls
fried foods	salad dressings (except for those given in this book)
gefilte fish	smoked fish or meat
gravy	soda, ginger ale, cola drinks
honey	sugar and syrups
ice cream	waffles
ices	yogurt
jam	

MENU PLAN FOR WOMEN

(See Rules for All Weight Watchers. Use all the foods in the specified amounts and only at the specified meals.)

BREAKFAST: 1 egg or 1 ounce hard cheese or 2 ounces fish
or ¼ cup cottage or pot cheese
1 slice enriched bread

LUNCHEON: 4 ounces fish (canned or fresh) or lean meat or
poultry or ⅔ cup (6 ounces) cottage
cheese or pot cheese or 4 ounces farmer
cheese or 2 ounces hard cheese or 2 eggs
All you want of unlimited vegetables (Chapter 6)
1 slice enriched bread

DINNER: 6 ounces cooked lean meat or fish or poultry
1 portion limited vegetable (Chapter 7)
All you want of unlimited vegetables

MUST BE TAKEN AT SOME TIME DURING DAY: A total of 3
fruits (one of them orange or grapefruit)
2 cups (16 ounces) skim milk or buttermilk or 1 cup
(8 ounces) skimmed evaporated milk

MAY BE TAKEN AT ANY TIME OF DAY: Any unlimited foods—
beverages, vegetables, etc.

MENU PLAN FOR MEN

(See Rules for All Weight Watchers. Use all the foods in the specified amounts and only at the specified meals.)

BREAKFAST: 1 egg or 1 ounce hard cheese or 2 ounces fish
or ¼ cup cottage or pot cheese
2 slices enriched bread

LUNCHEON: 4 ounces fish (canned or fresh) or lean meat or
poultry or ⅔ cup (6 ounces) cottage

cheese or pot cheese or 4 ounces farmer
cheese or 2 ounces hard cheese or 2 eggs
All you want of unlimited vegetables (Chapter 6)
2 slices enriched bread

DINNER: 8 ounces cooked lean meat or fish or poultry
1 portion limited vegetable (Chapter 7)
All you want of unlimited vegetables

MUST BE TAKEN AT SOME TIME DURING DAY: A total of 5
fruits (one of them orange or grapefruit)
2 cups (16 ounces) skim milk or buttermilk or 1 cup (8
ounces) skimmed evaporated milk
MAY BE TAKEN AT ANY TIME OF DAY: Any unlimited foods—
beverages, vegetables, etc.

MENU PLAN FOR TEENAGERS

(See Rules for All Weight Watchers. Use all the foods in the
specified amounts and only at the specified meals.)

BREAKFAST: 1 egg or 1 ounce hard cheese or 2 ounces fish
or ¼ cup cottage, pot or farmer cheese
1 slice enriched bread

LUNCHEON: 4 ounces fish (canned or fresh) or lean meat
or poultry or ⅔ cup (6 ounces) cottage
cheese or pot cheese or 4 ounces farmer
cheese or 2 ounces hard cheese or 2 eggs
All you want of unlimited vegetables (Chapter 6)
2 slices enriched bread

DINNER: 6 ounces cooked lean meat or fish or poultry
1 portion limited vegetable (Chapter 7)
All you want of unlimited vegetables
1 slice enriched bread

MUST BE TAKEN AT SOME TIME DURING DAY: A total of 5
fruits (one of them orange or grapefruit)
1 quart (32 ounces) skim milk or buttermilk

These may be used at meals, as after-school, TV-time
or bedtime snacks, etc., but be sure to use all your
fruits and all your milk each day.

MAY BE TAKEN AT ANY TIME OF DAY: Any unlimited foods—
beverages, vegetables. etc.

MENU SUGGESTIONS †

BREAKFAST

Half Cantaloupe
Eggs Sunny-Side Up on
Toast, p. 31

Tomato Juice
Asparagus Puff, p. 35
Toast

Pineapple Quarter
Two Ounces Tuna Fish
on Toast

Cottage Cheese (2 oz.)
Fresh Grapefruit Sections
Lettuce Bed
Toast

Grapefruit Sections
Egg in a Nest, p. 30
Milk Shake

Austrian Breakfast Pancake,
p. 42 (includes fruit and
bread)

Fresh Fruit Cup (½ cup)
Scrambled Egg W.W., p. 30
Toast

Quarter of Fresh Pineapple
Crab Meat (2 ounces, com-
bined with Chambord
Sauce, p. 219)
Toast

Broiled Half Grapefruit
Two Ounces Salmon
Toast

Fresh Juice of One Orange
One Ounce Cheese Melted
on Toast

Half Grapefruit
French Toast, p. 28

† Note: You may include legal beverage or fruit with each meal
but do not exceed amounts allowed by your Menu Plan.

TEEN-SCENE BREAKFASTS

French Toast, p. 28
Strawberry Smash (milk shake or malted made with 1 serving of strawberries)

Applesauce W.W., p. 249
Speedy Summer Breakfast, p. 37

LUNCHEON

Bean-Sprout Soup, p. 152
Four Ounces Shrimp
Toast

Black Mushroom Soup, p. 171
June Salad, p. 50
Apple Charlotte (includes bread), p. 246

Four Ounces Drained Tuna Fish, Mixed with Lettuce, Radishes, Celery and French-Style String Beans
Quick Tangy Dressing, p. 234
Toast

Cream of Asparagus and Mushroom Soup, p. 150
Mile-high Egg Salad Sandwich, p. 36
Pickles
Greens

Four Ounces Broiled Lobster Tail
Jellied Tomato Salad, p. 203
Asparagus on Toast

Quick Manhattan Clam Chowder, p. 61 (made with 2 ounces clams)
Vegetable Plate: Cooked Cauliflower, Green Beans and Asparagus, Covered with Cheese Sauce, p. 218
Toast

Asparagus Bouillon, p. 148
Cheese Soufflé, p. 47
Dilled Cucumber Slices, p. 161

Fresh Fruit Salad (⅛ pineapple, ¼ orange, 3 strawberries, cut up)
Cottage Cheese (3 ounces)
Sour Cream W.W., p. 233 (made with 3 ounces cottage cheese) *or* Golden Dressing, p. 226
Toast

Tomato Juice
Four Ounces Broiled Salmon with Oregano
Cucumber Sauce, p. 222, on Lettuce
Toast

TEEN-SCENE LUNCHES

Chiles Rellenas, p. 173
"Popcorn Bowl," p. 146
Toast
Apple Shake (shake in
    blender 1 serving of Ap-
    plesauce W.W., p. 249,
    with 1 cup of skim milk)

Tuna Pizza, p. 46
Ice Cream Soda, p. 271

Bean-Sprout Soup, p. 152
Eggs Foo Yung with Chicken,
    p. 35
Toast

EASY LUNCHES TO EAT OUT

Tuna or Salmon Platter
    (including lettuce and any
    unlimited vegetables)
Lemon Wedge

Four Ounces Sliced Turkey or
    Roast Beef
One Slice Bread

Cottage Cheese (6 ounces)
    and Cantaloupe or Other
    Fruit in Season
One Slice Bread

Broiled Hamburger
One Slice Toast
Relish

Two Eggs on Toast
Fruit

Melted Open Cheese
    Sandwich (on 1 slice Toast)
Fruit

Tomato Juice
Broiled Fish (4 ounces)
Lemon Wedge
Hearts of Lettuce
Toast

FISH DINNERS

Bean-Sprout Soup, p. 152
Broiled Red Snapper
Asparagus
Brussels Sprouts

Swordfish Diablo, p. 90
Chinese Vegetable
Mushrooms
Lemon Gelatin, p. 252

Tomato Bouillon, p. 199
Butterfly Shrimp Scampi,
    p. 84, Parsley Garnish
Large Tossed Salad, Spicy
    Salad Dressing, p. 235
Eggplant

Curried Cream of Kale Soup,
    p. 165
Broiled Trout
Carrots
Broiled Mushrooms, p. 167
Half Cup Stewed Fruit

Jellied Madrilene, p. 206
Barbecued or Broiled Lobster
    Tails, p. 76 (seasoned with
    BBQ Baste, p. 216)
Broccoli
Cooked Artichoke or Peas
Pineapple Kabobs

Mock Split-Pea Soup
    (made without carrots
    and onions), p. 164
Broiled Fillet of Sole *or*
    Easy Baked Fish with
    Tomato Sauce, p. 72
Beets
Mushroom "Mychele," p. 166
Lemon Gelatin, p. 252

Sea Food Platter:
    Artichoke Stuffed with
        3 Ounces Crab Meat, p. 184
    Lobster Waldorf Salad, p. 93
    (see your Menu Plan for
        allowed amount)
    Sea Food Cocktail Sauce,
        p. 235
Cooked Cauliflower
Chilled Spiced Rhubarb,
    p. 175

BEEF DINNERS

Stuffed Peppers, p. 108 (this
    includes 2 ounces cooked
    meat—reduce steak accord-
    ingly)
Broiled Steak, p. 96
Cold String Bean Stew, p. 163
Red Cabbage Relish, p. 154

Cabbage Soup, p. 154
Hungarian Goulash, p. 101
Lemon Gelatin, p. 252

Curried Cream of Kale Soup,
    p. 165
Beef and Eggplant Casserole,
    p. 98
Relish Tray of Celery Sticks,
    Radish Flowers, Parsley
Water-Cress Salad
    Dressing, p. 237

Fruit Cup
Boiled Beef Dinner in One
    Pot, p. 102
Mustard Pickle
Tomato Aspic, p. 204
Baked Rhubarb, p. 175

Black Mushroom Soup, p. 171
Chinese Beef and Cabbage
    Casserole, p. 98 (includes
    limited vegetable)
Any Unlimited Vegetables
Kumquats, p. 252

Braised Beef Roll-Ups, p. 102
Cucumber Salad
Blender Basil Dressing,
    p. 217
Strawberry Ice, p. 263

Chilled Chicken Consommé
    and Cucumber Refresher,
    p. 160
Beef Ragout W.W., p. 101
Mushrooms as desired
Ginger Melon Mold, p. 255

VEAL DINNERS

Borsht, p. 186
Broiled Veal Chops, p. 112,
    with Mushrooms
Half Cup Stewed Spinach
Lettuce Wedges, Thousand
    Island Dressing, p. 237

Spinach and Romaine Soup,
    p. 177
Vealburgers, p. 111
Chinese Sweet and Sour Sauce,
    p. 223
Salad Tossed with French-
    Style Green Beans
Tomato French Dressing,
    p. 236

Hot Consommé
Continental Veal, p. 117
Tossed Green Salad, p. 146
Strawberry Parfait, p. 272

LIVER DINNERS

Spinach Soup with Fine Herbs
    p. 178
Calves Liver Alla Veneziana,
    p. 125 (includes limited
    vegetable)
Red Cabbage Relish, p. 154
Pineapple and Rhubarb
    Compote, p. 262

Liver Broiled with Sautéed
    Onion Flakes, Salt and
    Mushrooms
Carrots
Minted Melon, p. 252

LAMB DINNER

Turkish Eggplant Caviar
  (½ cup), p. 192
Broiled Lamb Chops *or* Roast
  Leg of Lamb
Broiled Pineapple Slices
Mint Sauce, p. 229
Salad Bowl of Unlimited
  Vegetables
Thousand Island Dressing,
  p. 237

FRANKFURTER DINNERS

Frankfurter Casserole Creole
  Style, p. 133
Cole Slaw, p. 153

Mock Split-Pea Soup, p. 164
Barbecued Frankfurters-
  Sauerkraut, p. 132
Greens with Radishes and
  Cucumbers
Mustard Dressing, p. 231
Lemon Gelatin, p. 252

POULTRY DINNERS

Black Mushroom Soup, p. 171
Paella, p. 139
Herbed Zucchini, p. 180
Salad
Any Unlimited Salad Dressing
Fresh Berries

Asparagus Bouillon, p. 148
Broiled Chicken
Cauliflower
Peas
Perfection Salad, p. 145
Baked Apple, p. 248

Turkey (light meat)
Jellied Cranberry Sauce, p. 251
Broccoli
Squash
Grape Whip, p. 250

Escarole Soup, p. 162
Chicken Cacciatora, p. 135
Broiled Mushrooms
Herbed Zucchini, p. 180
Maple Bavarian Cream, p. 274

MENUS FOR SPECIAL OCCASIONS AND SNACKS

AFTER-SHOPPING PARTY

Serve hot bouillon in gay casseroles or mugs surrounded by bowls of minced herbs such as parsley, chives or oregano. Fragrant and refreshing.

MILK BAR

Eight ounces skim milk sweetened with liquid sugar substitute, flavored with vanilla extract. Serve straight or on the rocks, or shake up in jar and serve frothy.

PICNIC PARTY

Believe me, it's no picnic to be a "chubby bubby" in the summer. So forget the potato salad, frankfurter rolls and doughnuts and stick to your W.W. Program. Try my Cole Slaw made with Mustard Dressing (p. 231).

THE PLAY WAS WONDERFUL

Invite everyone in for an after-theater nightcap. Serve chilled tomato juice in sparkling crystal goblets, Orange Delight (p. 256), a non-caloric carbonated drink, and café espresso brewed in one of the table-size machines in the living room. Or, feature a soup bar— three or four legal soups from our "Unlimited Vegetable" chapter— a green one, a red (tomato), and a pale consommé, all piping hot. And be sure to introduce them as Weight Watchers specials.

THE COCKTAIL HOUR

No, we do not permit alcoholic beverages in the Weight Watchers Program, but you can enjoy an hour or two of relaxation with company, serving glasses of tomato juice, non-caloric carbonated drinks of your own choice, "Roast Peanuts," p. 170, the "Popcorn Bowl," p. 146, and Stewed Rhubarb, p. 175. Your daily fruit or malted milk can be taken at this time if you like but most people prefer to have it for a nightcap.

COFFEE BREAK

To make iced coffee, put into blender 1 heaping teaspoonful instant coffee, ½ teaspoon sugar substitute, 2 ice cubes and 1 cup water. Blend till frothy. Serve in tall glass. Or put ice cubes in glass and pour other blended ingredients over them.

CAFE SOCIETY

You already belong to a society—the overweight society. Follow your W.W. Program and stick to your legal foods.

RULES FOR USING EGGS

Limit egg intake to 4-7 per week. Eggs are allowed only at breakfast or luncheon, not at dinner.

We have great admiration for both the egg and the chicken. To us, however, there is no question but that the egg comes first, at least in the day's menu. So we open our recipe section to the noble product of the busy hen.

First
Beat one egg ... soak one slice of white bread in egg

Second
Heavy iron skillet

After skillet is very hot add slice of soaked bread. Brown on both sides.

FRENCH TOAST IN A DRY SKILLET

Soak 1 slice *bread in one well-beaten *egg. Heat heavy iron skillet and when very hot add soaked bread. Brown on both sides. This is faster than broiling but many Weight Watchers prefer the broiling method.

BROILED FRENCH TOAST

Soak 1 slice *bread in one well-beaten *egg. Broil or bake on tin foil. Sprinkle cinnamon and sugar substitute on top. Return to oven or broiler to melt cinnamon if desired. *Apples or other allowed *fruit may be broiled too, and served with French toast.

STRAWBERRY TOPPING FOR FRENCH TOAST

A half cup of fresh *strawberries mashed well and seasoned with few drops of vanilla flavor or orange extract and sugar substitute to taste. Count as 1 fruit.

FRENCH TOAST—"TWO FERS"

In the idiom of show business "two fers" are two tickets sold for the price of one. This is a Weight Watchers version of theatrical leger-demain.

*1 egg
  2 teaspoons water
  ⅛ teaspoon salt
  ⅛ teaspoon MSG
*1 slice white bread, cut in half with serrated bread
    knife to make 2 thin slices
  1 package granulated sugar substitute
  ¼ teaspoon cinnamon

Beat egg, water, salt and MSG. Dip bread into egg and brown on both sides in non-stick skillet or on a grill. Use spatula to turn bread as it is too thin to handle with a fork. This makes 2 slices of French toast (which almost double in bulk during cooking). Sprinkle with cinnamon sugar made by mixing granulated sugar substitute with cinnamon.

FRENCH TOAST IN QUANTITY

You can make French toast for breakfast even for a large family by this simple method. For each serving, break an *egg into a shallow ovenproof dish. Beat a few drops of water into the egg, then soak a slice of *bread for each serving overnight in the egg mix, turning once. Next morning slip the dish holding the egg into a 375-400°F. oven, or transfer all the slices to a large shallow oven tray. Cook until top is puffy and brown.

BOILING EGGS

There are many different systems for boiling *eggs but using this cold-water start I almost never have to contend with cracked eggs.

* *Limited food—see Menu Plan, p. 18-20, for legal amount.*

Lower an egg into a white enamel pan (egg will stain aluminum) and cover it with cool tap water. Then cook it gently. To get a soft-set yolk and firm white, allow 6 minutes (5-minute egg when you start with boiling water).

Hard-boiled eggs will need 15 minutes. As soon as eggs are done, plunge them into cold water so they shell easily.

POACHING EGGS

Use a small saucepan of water, add a little salt and 1 tablespoon vinegar, open *eggs in a cup and slide them into the simmering water. When done, remove them with a slotted spoon and drain them on a clean dry towel. Serve at once or keep warm in a dish set in a pan of water. 2½-3 minutes of gentle poaching will produce softly-set eggs. 5 minutes, hard set eggs.

WAYS TO SERVE POACHED EGGS, W.W.

Poach very large mushroom caps 3 minutes in boiling water containing lemon juice. Put a poached egg in each one. Cover with Chambord Sauce (see index for recipe) and sprinkle with paprika.

EGGS IN A NEST

Did you ever have these? Children like them, I like them too. Lightly brown one slice of *bread in toaster. Tear out center section (save it for making bread crumbs) and lay remaining bread in hot skillet. Drop a *whole egg into the depression (if the egg breaks, use it for something else), cover skillet and let cook until egg is set. For a firmer egg, turn once.

SCRAMBLED EGGS

You know about scrambling *eggs? Just beat them in a bowl with a few teaspoons of water to fluff them up (yes, water is unlimited) and pour into a preheated heavy skillet. Stir until you get egg as you like it.

There's no law against dropping the open egg into a preheated pan, and *then* beating with a fork.

Season scrambled eggs with chopped pimento.

One nice way to serve scrambled eggs is with some cut-up cooked asparagus tips.

Ever think of adding drained bean sprouts?

Eggs may be scrambled with *cottage cheese, but the cheese must be counted. To serve two for luncheon, scramble 3 eggs with 3 ounces cottage cheese.

EGG LOUISIANA

    1 green pepper, diced
    2 teaspoons dehydrated onion flakes, cut up
   *2 eggs, beaten
    Seasoning to taste

Steam pepper and onion in water for approximately 15 minutes. Pour beaten eggs over steamed vegetables and bake in oven for approximately 15 minutes.

SUNNY-SIDE UP

Heat a small heavy skillet without adding fat. Break an *egg into skillet. Cook until sides begin to brown. Serve as is (with moist top) or turn with spatula to brown second side.

To firm top without turning, cover skillet with small heatproof plate and serve when set as you like.

MAKING A BASIC FAT-FREE OMELET

Even a one-egg omelet can be made without added fat if you use a heavy small pan. Contrary to many cookbook directions, I do not have a pan exclusively for omelets but use a heavy 5-inch skillet. I pre-heat the pan, beat up one *egg (two at luncheon), add a few drops of water (turn on the tap in the kitchen sink, turn it off, and catch the few drops that leak out). When the pan is smoking hot, I add the egg, turn down the heat to moderate and let the egg cook on the bottom, lifting the edges slightly so that the uncooked portion runs to the bottom.

When the bottom is brown, you can add filling, or turn the omelet onto your plate, or let it continue to cook until the top is dry (as I do; I have a prejudice against runny eggs).

Serve the egg flipped over in half, so you know you're eating an omelet.

Add few drops of water while beating egg

get 5", heavy, skillet very hot.
Add egg and brown bottom. Then turn down heat and cook until top is done the way you like it.

Serve folded over so it looks like an omelet.

SPANISH OMELET

Heat a heavy 6-inch frypan. Pour in *1 beaten egg and cook on a medium flame until set on one side, turn, add a tablespoon of Creole Sauce (see index for recipe) and cook until second side is set. Fold omelet in half and serve.

OMELET AU JOUR

  *2 eggs, well beaten
  Salt
  Pepper
  MSG
  Any unlimited vegetables (see index)

Pour beaten, seasoned eggs into hot skillet. When eggs are set at bottom but moist on top, pour cooked vegetables over them. Place under broiler until omelet doubles in bulk and is cooked through, about 5 minutes.

The omelet can be made from any unlimited vegetable: broccoli, cauliflower, string beans, etc. This is also a wonderful way to use up leftover vegetables, since 2 or 3 kinds may be used on the same omelet. If one egg is used for luncheon a slice of *cheese (1 ounce) may be placed on top of vegetables and egg just before placing under broiler. Cooked green pepper and dehydrated onion flakes (soaked in water or *skim milk) make a very tasty omelet mixed with other vegetables or used alone.

SPINACH OMELET

Beat ½ package slightly defrosted chopped spinach into *2 eggs. Add diced mushrooms if desired, salt and pepper. Cook in non-stick pan or hot skillet.

  * Limited food—see Menu Plan, p. 18-20, for legal amount.

OMELET AND SALAD BOUQUET

Combine ¼ cup crisp celery and ¼ cup green pepper. Heat quickly in water. Don't cook them, they should stay crisp. Drain, add a tablespoon of chopped chives, season with salt and pepper and fold into omelet.

CHINESE VEGETABLE OMELET FOR ONE

    1½ tablespoons dehydrated onion flakes
    1½ tablespoons finely diced celery
    1½ tablespoons finely diced green pepper
    1 tablespoon bean sprouts
    ¼ cup bouillon, chicken stock or water
  *1 egg

Heat a heavy aluminum skillet and as soon as hot put in vegetables. They will brown quickly. Add bouillon, chicken stock or water and let vegetables cook until soft and liquid is absorbed. Cook for another minute, stirring constantly. Heat a small 6-inch iron skillet. Add the vegetable mixture. Beat egg and put into skillet. Cook until omelet is brown on one side. Turn, brown second side. Serve hot.

EGGS FOO YUNG

    ¾ pound mushrooms
    2 tablespoons chicken stock
    ¼ cup dehydrated onion flakes, soaked in water
    1 cup diced celery
    ¾ cup bean sprouts, drained
  *4 eggs
    ¼ teaspoon salt
    ⅛ teaspoon pepper

Cook for 1 minute the sliced mushrooms in the 2 tablespoons chicken stock. Add onions and celery, stir and sauté for 5 minutes. Cool.

Add drained bean sprouts. Beat eggs until light. Add salt and pepper and cooled vegetables. Heat small iron skillet and when very hot add a large spoonful of mixture, enough to make 4-inch cakes. When pancakes are brown on bottom, turn and brown second side. Serve immediately with soy sauce. Luncheon for two.

EGG FOO YUNG MADE WITH MEAT

    *1 egg
     ¼ cup bean sprouts
    *2 ounces shredded white meat of chicken or
        turkey, or lean roast beef
     Onion flakes
     Dash of salt and pepper

Beat egg and combine with bean sprouts and chicken, turkey or beef. Heat a heavy iron skillet until it is smoking hot. Pour in egg mixture and cook just as you would any pancake. When it is brown on one side, flip it over and do the other one. You can add ⅛ teaspoon of soy sauce to the original egg mix.

ASPARAGUS PUFF

     1 cup cut-up cooked asparagus
    *1 tablespoon bread crumbs (whiz crusts from
        allowed bread in blender)
    *1 egg, beaten
    *1 cup skim milk
     ⅛ teaspoon sugar substitute
     Salt

Mix asparagus, bread crumbs, beaten egg and milk; stir well. Add sugar substitute and salt and place in baking dish. Bake in moderate oven at 350°F. until firm, but not dry. One-half luncheon.

SPINACH AND MUSHROOM SOUFFLE

½ cup Cream of Spinach Soup W.W. (see index
  for recipe)
¼ cup canned sliced mushrooms
*1 egg, separated

In an individual casserole combine soup, mushrooms and egg yolk.
Mix well. Beat white of egg until it is stiff; fold into mixture in
casserole. Bake at 350°F. for half an hour. An excellent Sunday
breakfast dish.

MILE-HIGH EGG SALAD SANDWICH

*2 hard-cooked eggs, finely chopped
 2 tablespoons chopped pickles or pickle relish
 ¼ cup finely diced celery
 2 tablespoons finely diced green pepper
 1 tablespoon chopped parsley
 Allowed salad dressing to taste (see salad dressing
   chapter)
 Salt, pepper and mustard added to taste

Combine all ingredients and pile up on allowed bread.

CREAMED MUSHROOMS AND EGGS

¼ pound fresh mushrooms
2 teaspoons onion flakes, soaked in water
¼ cup beef stock
*2 hard-boiled eggs, sliced

Heat heavy aluminum skillet over low flame. Add mushrooms cut
vertically, onion flakes and beef stock. Cover pan and cook until
tender but do not let mushrooms become too dry. When cool, chop,
add *milk or stock if necessary, reheat, and sprinkle over sliced eggs.

VEGETABLE CUTLET

Cooked unlimited vegetables
*2 eggs, beaten
*1 slice of bread (or use soggy bread and squeeze
   out water)

Combine ingredients. Make patty and put in broiler, or brown in hot
dry skillet, turning once.

SPEEDY SUMMER BREAKFAST

2 envelopes granulated sugar substitute
*1 egg
*1 cup buttermilk
1 tablespoon lemon juice
1 small strip of lemon peel

Put everything into the blender and run for about half a minute.
Serve cold.

BAKED CUP CUSTARD

*1 egg lightly beaten
1¼ teaspoons liquid sugar substitute
*1 cup skim milk
Pinch of salt
¼ teaspoon vanilla
Dash of cinnamon

Combine egg with sugar substitute. Slowly add milk, salt and vanilla,
blending well. Pour mixture into 2 custard cups. Sprinkle with
cinnamon. Bake in pan of hot water, about 1 hour, in 325°F. oven.
Two luncheon servings. One may be saved for the following day.
Count milk. Good with the following menu:

Open-Faced Sandwiches
    Each one made from 2 ounces of *tuna fish, cut-up
    asparagus, and Pimento French Dressing
Tomato Aspic, p. 204
Ball of Cottage Cheese (1½ oz.)
Baked Cup Custard

TOP-OF-STOVE CUSTARD

    *1 egg lightly beaten
    1 teaspoon granulated sugar substitute
    *1 cup skim milk
    ½ teaspoon vanilla
    Grated nutmeg

Combine beaten egg with sugar substitute. Stir in skim milk and
vanilla. Blend well. Pour into two custard cups. Sprinkle with nutmeg. Set custard cups in pan holding hot water. Cook at top of stove
for 1 hour until knife inserted in center comes out clean. Delicious!

CUSTARD SAUCE

    *⅔ cup skim milk
    *2 egg yolks
    Dash salt
    ½ teaspoon vanilla or rum extract
    2 packets granulated sugar substitute

Scald milk in double boiler. Beat egg yolks with salt; add milk, a
little at a time, stirring constantly. Return to double boiler and cook
over hot (not boiling) water, stirring constantly, until mixture coats
the spoon. Remove from hot water; stir in extract and sugar substitute. Cool, then refrigerate until well chilled. Makes 2 servings.
Good over peach slices (one portion of fruit).

RULES FOR USING CHEESE

Cheese is allowed only at breakfast or luncheon, not at dinner. At breakfast, 1 ounce hard cheese or ¼ cup cottage cheese or pot cheese may be used, following your Menu Plan. At luncheon, 2 ounces hard cheese or ⅔ cup cottage or pot cheese may be used, following your Menu Plan.

HARD CHEESE—2 OUNCES

You may have 2 ounces hard cheese for lunch. The following are classified as hard cheeses. Not all of them will be available in your part of the country but enough will be.

American	Gjetast	Reggiano
Appetitost	Gruyere	Romano
Apple	Kumminost	Sapsago
Asiago	Muenster ‡	Sardo
Cheddar	Nokkelost	Shrinz
Cheshire	Parmesan	Swiss †
Edam †	Provolone	

† Has lower fat content than American cheese.
‡ Actually a semi-soft cheese, but we permit its use.

COTTAGE CHEESE

Cottage cheese is a soft white cheese made by straining and seasoning the curds of milk. Two ounces (4 tablespoons) are allowed at breakfast. Six ounces (⅔ cup) are allowed at lunch. Since difference in fat between regular cottage cheese and skim milk cottage cheese is negligible, you may use the regular cottage cheese.

POT CHEESE

Pot cheese is almost identical in content (not texture) to cottage cheese. Use interchangeably—⅔ cup or 6 ounces at lunch.

FARMER CHEESE

Available only in some sections of the country, this is a pressed form of cottage cheese. Use interchangeably, but in slightly reduced amounts because it is compressed. We allow ½ cup at luncheon.

* *Limited food—see Menu Plan, p. 18-20, for legal amount.*

CHEESE APPETIZERS

  *2 ounces grated American cheese
   Paprika
   Whole cloves

Shape grated American cheese into small balls. Dip one end into paprika. Stick whole clove and clove stem into opposite end. Bake at 350°F. and serve to two. Count each serving as ½ luncheon dish. Use for an attractive company luncheon. Here is one menu possibility:

> *Cheese Appetizers,* chilled
> *Asparagus Bisque* (see index)
> *Open-Faced Roast Beef Sandwiches for Two*
>   Each made with 2 ounces lean *beef
> *Pineapple Quarters*
> *Beverage*

CHEESE FONDUE

  *1 egg
  *½ cup skim milk or tomato juice
  *1 slice bread
  *¼ cup hard cheese, diced (1 ounce)
   Salt
   Pepper
   Chopped parsley
   Onion salt

Beat egg. Add milk or tomato juice, bread, cheese and seasonings. Bake in moderate oven 350°F. until firm in center, about 20-30 minutes. Good for a change.

AUSTRIAN BREAKFAST PANCAKE

*2 ounces cottage cheese
*1 slice white enriched bread, cut up
 Water (or *skim milk) to start blender
*½ apple or peach
 Cinnamon and sugar substitute

Heat a 5-inch skillet. Meanwhile put into blender cottage cheese, bread, and enough water or skim milk to start the blender. Blend thoroughly. Pour batter into *hot* skillet and cook until brown on bottom. Do not turn. Pare, core and slice an apple or peach and cut into very thin slices. Sprinkle fruit generously over the pancake (one-quarter or one-half of the fruit is the way I do it). Transfer skillet to broiler, set at least 4 inches from heat and broil until fruit is done and top is brown. Sprinkle with cinnamon and sugar substitute (the latter can be put under broiler to melt). *Blueberries, *strawberries, *orange sections, etc., may be used to replace apple.

Pour batter into 5" skillet... brown on bottom. Do not turn.

Add thinly sliced fruit.

Place in broiler 4" from heat. Remove when golden brown.

CHEESE BLINTZES

*3 eggs
 2 tablespoons water

Beat eggs and water. Make thin pancakes using 3 tablespoons batter in small non-stick pan. Tip pan in all directions to make even layer of batter. Brown only 1 side and turn out on clean cloth.

FILLING

*⅔ cup cottage cheese
*1 egg, beaten
 Small piece of orange rind
 Sugar substitute

Combine filling ingredients; mash well. Put a heaping tablespoon on the edge of browned side of each pancake. Roll up, tuck in ends. Broil or bake both sides in hot oven 10-15 minutes. Serves 3 at luncheon (1 portion cheese, 2 portions eggs).

CHEESE DIP #1

> ½ teaspoon dehydrated onion, soaked in water
>   for 5 minutes
> 2 radishes
> ½ stalk celery
> 1 slice green pepper
> 1 vegetable bouillon cube
> Dash garlic powder
> *⅔ cup cottage or pot cheese

Liquefy onion, water in which it was soaked and all other ingredients in blender. Store in refrigerator for 2 hours to thicken. Serve as a luncheon dip using celery stalks, endive and other greens as dippers. If divided into 4 portions, each containing ¼ of allowed luncheon cheese, supplement with 3 ounces (¾ portion) fish per serving to complete the meal.

Worcestershire sauce, 1 tsp.
Tabasco sauce, dash.

6 ozs. creamed cottage cheese.
4 oz. can pimentos
⅛ tsp. salt.
⅛ tsp. garlic salt.

Place ingredients in blender and purée until smooth.
Serve as dip for sticks of fresh vegetables!

CHEESE DIP #2

    *3 ounces cottage cheese
    *1 tablespoon skim milk
    ½ small clove garlic
    ¼ teaspoon salt
    ¼ teaspoon paprika
    1 teaspoon Worcestershire sauce

Place all ingredients in blender container and blend 20 seconds. Refrigerate until ready to use. A good dip for unlimited vegetables.

COTTAGE CHEESE ON TOAST

    *2 ounces cottage cheese
    *1 slice white bread, enriched
    Sugar substitute
    Cinnamon

Spread cottage cheese on white bread. Add a few drops sugar substitute to cottage cheese if desired, and sprinkle with cinnamon. Bake on tin foil in 375° F. oven. Breakfast for one.

GRILLED CHEESE AND TUNA

    *2 ounces drained tuna
    *1 slice white bread
    *1 ounce any hard cheese, cut up

Spread tuna on shallow ovenproof platter over 1 slice white bread. Put cheese on top. Bake at 350° F. or broil until cheese is melted. Use for lunch.

PIZZA

> *1 slice white bread
> *Tomato sauce (tomato juice cooked down to half
>   its volume)
> *2 ounces hard cheese, cut up
>   Oregano or garlic powder

Toast bread, spread lightly with tomato sauce, put cheese on top and sprinkle with oregano or garlic powder. Broil until cheese is melted.

TUNA PIZZA

Follow recipe above but use only *1½ ounces hard cheese. Dot pizza with 1 ounce *tuna fish and seasonings. Broil.

CHEESE AND CUCUMBER SAUCE

> 2 cucumbers, chopped very fine
> 2 tablespoons lemon juice
> *⅓ cup cottage cheese
> 1 teaspoon grated onion or sautéed onion powder
> 1 teaspoon salt
> Pepper

Place in blender and purée. Serve as luncheon for two over 6 ounces crab meat. Or serve half of sauce (for one) over 3 ounces crab meat and store other half in refrigerator.

CHEESE AND MUSHROOM CASSEROLE

Sauté ½ pound mushrooms in 3 tablespoons of chicken or beef stock. Put into small casserole. Add *2 ounces hard cheese with *½ cup bread crumbs (made from 1 slice bread whizzed in blender). Bake at 350° F. until brown. Serves 1.

CHEESE SOUFFLE

*½ cup skim milk
*1 ounce sharp cheddar cheese, grated
*1 slice bread, cut up
 ⅓ teaspoon salt
 Dash paprika
 Dash dry mustard
 A whisper of cayenne pepper
*1 egg, separated

Heat milk (do not boil), add cheese, bread and seasonings. As soon as cheese is melted remove from heat and stir in beaten egg yolk. Fold in well-beaten egg whites. Put into small casserole and bake at 350° F. until puffed and brown. Serves 1 at luncheon.

CHEESE MOLD

 1 envelope unflavored gelatin
*½ cup cold skim milk
*1 cup Whipped Topping W.W.
*4 ounces grated hard cheese
 1 teaspoon Worcestershire sauce
 ½ teaspoon dry mustard
 Dash cayenne pepper
 ½ teaspoon paprika
 Mixed greens

Soften gelatin in skim milk. Combine the rest of ingredients except greens. Heat gelatin over hot water until dissolved. Add to Whipped Topping-cheese mixture. Pour into a wet ring mold and refrigerate until set. Unmold and fill center with greens. Pass a bowl of Tomato French Dressing W.W. (see index for recipe). 2 servings at lunch (count ¾ cup skim milk in each one).

CHEESE-STUFFED CELERY

>   Celery stalks
> *3 ounces cottage cheese
>   1 can mushrooms
>   Salt and pepper
>   Parsley flakes
>   Dehydrated onion flakes (if desired), soaked
>   in water

Clean celery and stuff with remaining blended ingredients. Carry for lunch with one hard-cooked egg and slice of enriched bread.

CHEESE ASPIC-SHRIMP PATIO PLATTER FOR A BRIDGE LUNCHEON

CHEESE LAYER

>   1 envelope unflavored gelatin
> *1 cup skim milk
>   ½ teaspoon salt
>   2 teaspoons instant onion
> *6 ounces cottage cheese
> *¾ cup buttermilk
>   2 tablespoons lemon juice
>   1 teaspoon Worcestershire sauce
>   1 cup thinly sliced red radishes

Sprinkle gelatin on milk in saucepan. Stir constantly over low heat, about 3 minutes, until gelatin dissolves. Remove from heat. Stir in salt and onion. Soften cheese in whipping bowl and blend in buttermilk until smooth; stir in lemon juice and Worcestershire sauce. Gradually stir in gelatin mixture, beating until smooth. Chill, stirring occasionally, until mixture mounds when topped from spoon. Fold in radishes; turn into 9 x 5 x 3-loaf pan. Chill firm. Now you are ready to make . . .

* Limited food—see Menu Plan, p. 18-20, for legal amount.

*... this makes a very festive dish,
your "bridge ladies" will love it ...
and save their waist lines at
the same time.*

TOMATO ASPIC LAYER

   3 envelopes unflavored gelatin
   2 cups cold water
 *3 cups tomato juice
   1 tablespoon lemon juice
   1 teaspoon Worcestershire sauce
   ¼ teaspoon Tabasco sauce

Sprinkle gelatin on 1½ cups cold water in 2-quart saucepan. Stir constantly over low heat, about 3 minutes, until gelatin dissolves. Remove from heat; stir in remaining ½ cup water and other ingredients. Let cool. Pour over almost-firm cheese layer. Chill firm. Unmold. Serve with allowed cooked shrimp marinated in Tangy Herb Dressing W.W. minus 1 lunch portion for cottage cheese in Cheese Aspic or 28 ounces of cooked shrimp. This will make a very satisfying and festive main dish. Serves 8. Note: Each serving uses about ¼ cup daily milk allowance, and 6 ounces of tomato juice.

JUNE SALAD

    *⅔ cup cottage cheese
    *½ cup skim milk
    1 teaspoon salt
    1 tablespoon paprika
    2 tablespoons lemon juice
    ½ garlic clove
    ½ green pepper cut into strips
    4 radishes

Put all ingredients into blender. Cover. Blend at high speed 10 seconds. Serves 1 at luncheon over greens.

SPRING SALAD

    *⅔ cup cottage or pot cheese
    ½ cup Pimento French dressing
       (see index for recipe)
    Cut-up radish, cucumber, celery and green pepper

Blend cheese and sauce at high speed. Transfer to bowl. Add cut-up fresh vegetables. Serve with crisp toast for a delicious luncheon for one.

LAZY DAY CHEESE BLINTZES

    *3 slices white bread (cut in half horizontally)
    Cinnamon
    Granulated sugar substitute
    *⅔ cup cottage cheese
    *1 egg
    ½ teaspoon salt
    *1⅓ cups cottage cheese made into Sour Cream
       W.W. (see index)

Cut crusts from bread and with a rolling pin roll each slice. Sprinkle with cinnamon and sugar substitute. Mash cheese with fork, add egg and salt and mix well. Put a heaping tablespoon of cheese mixture in center of slice and pinch ends together with fingers. Put in wax paper and refrigerate until ready to use. Brown under broiler. Serve with Sour Cream W.W. Serves 3.

GOOD SAUCE FOR BLINTZES

Purée *raspberries in a blender or mash them fine. Strain or not, as you wish. Add sugar substitute and rum flavoring; serve as side dish for blintzes. Count as 1 fruit.

"DANISH PASTRY" LUNCHEON

> *1 slice enriched white bread
> *6 ounces pot cheese
> Water
> *1 fruit (¼ pineapple)
> Sugar substitute
> Cinnamon
> Varied flavoring extracts: orange, vanilla, rum, etc.

Toast the bread until it is golden. Lay it on a flat surface, and cut through the middle with a serrated knife to give you two slices of bread. Cut these in half, making 4 triangles. Mash 2 tablespoons of pot cheese with a teaspoon water, sweeten with sugar substitute and flavor with cinnamon. Pile on untoasted side of a triangle of toast, covering all of the top. Mash 2 tablespoons pot cheese with water, fold in finely diced pieces of pineapple, and sweeten with sugar substitute and orange extract. Pile on untoasted side of a second triangle of toast. Continue until you have used most of the cheese, adding your own flavorings as you wish. Put the 4 triangles of toast under the broiler (or in a hot oven) and heat for a few minutes until tops toast lightly. Use as dessert, and if there is any cheese left, be sure to eat it since on the Weight Watchers program you must use the allotted foods at each meal.

Note: *Whipped topping with *Applesauce W.W. folded into it makes a good spread for the toast; the topping and the applesauce must be counted toward your daily skim milk and fruit allowance.

COTTAGE CHEESE DANISH

   *1 slice crisp toast
   *2 ounces cottage cheese (breakfast allowance)
   ⅛ teaspoon cinnamon
   ⅛ teaspoon vanilla
   ½ package granulated sugar substitute

Mix cottage cheese with cinnamon, vanilla and sugar substitute. Spread on toast and place under broiler until warmed through. We think this tastes like a fresh-baked cheese Danish.

VARIATION

Use artificial butter flavor instead of vanilla and add ¼ teaspoon orange rind. Roll freshly-made toast with rolling pin to flatten, cut diagonally in half. Divide cheese mixture over toast halves, secure bread with toothpicks and bake in preheated oven, 500° F. for 10 minutes.

CREAM-CHEESE PIE

   *18 ounces cottage cheese
   ½ teaspoon nutmeg
   ¼ teaspoon cinnamon
   ½ teaspoon rum flavoring
   ½ teaspoon vanilla
   1½ teaspoons liquid sugar substitute
   *2 eggs, separated

Beat all ingredients except egg whites at high speed in electric beater or with rotary beater until smooth. Do not underbeat. Fold in stiffly beaten egg whites. Place in pie pan (7 inches). Set on bottom shelf of broiler rack. Broil 8 minutes or until top is golden brown. Serve hot or, even better, cold. Sliced *strawberries may be placed on top just before serving. Yield: 4 luncheon portions. Count fruit if used. May be refrigerated for several days.

Arithmetic: Cottage cheese totals 3 luncheon servings. Eggs total 1 luncheon serving.

NO COOKING CHIFFON CHEESECAKE

    1 envelope unflavored gelatin
    2 tablespoons lemon juice
    ½ cup hot water
 *2 eggs, separated
    2½ teaspoons sugar substitute
 *18 ounces cottage cheese
    1 cup crushed ice (easiest way is to wrap ice cubes
       in towel and crush with hammer)

Sprinkle gelatin on lemon juice placed in blender container. Add hot water, egg yolks, sugar substitute, cheese and crushed ice. Turn blender on high speed and run until well blended. Fold in egg whites, beaten until they form peaks. Chill until set—this sets very gradually. Luncheon—4 servings. Very easy, very good.

Note: Cheesecake may be topped with ½ cup *bread crumbs (1 slice bread whizzed in blender with ½ teaspoon granulated sugar substitute and a piece of grated orange rind).

LUNCHEON FOR TWO

Mock Split-Pea Soup, p. 164; *Creamed Mushrooms*, p. 167, on Toast; *No-Cooking Chiffon Cheese Cake; Beverage.*

CHEESE DIVAN

    1 4-oz. can mushrooms
    1 cup cooked broccoli
  *1 slice bread
  *2 ounces hard cheese, cut up

Place mushrooms, broccoli and bread in aluminum-foil pan side by side. Cover with hard cheese and broil until cheese melts. Serves 1.

PAPRIKA CHEESE BALLS

  *1 tablespoon nonfat dry milk solids
    1 tablespoon paprika
  *9 ounces cottage cheese
  *1 egg
    Salt and pepper to taste
    6-10 sprigs curly parsley

Mix the dry milk with paprika. Add to cheese and mash well. Break in egg and mix smooth. Add pepper to taste. Form into 1-inch balls. Sprinkle thin layer of salt on pan. Bake or broil the balls rolling them occasionally to brown all sides and avoid sticking. Balls may also be browned in a heated skillet over a flame. Garnish each cheese ball with a sprig of parsley. 2 luncheon servings. Serve with platter of cooked (unlimited) vegetables.

Note: Arithmetic check—1 egg equals half luncheon; 9 ounces cottage cheese equals 1½ luncheons; total, 2 luncheons.

    * Limited food—see Menu Plan, p. 18-20, for legal amount.

Fish

RULES FOR USING FISH

A minimum of 5 weekly fish meals (luncheons or dinners), from Group A. This does not preclude your having fish more often, and at breakfast also. Follow your Menu Plan, making your selection from the following, and changing frequently.

GROUP A		
	haddock	sturgeon (fresh)
abalone	hake	swordfish
bass	halibut	trout, brook
bluefish	lobster	trout, lake
bonito	mullet	tuna fish (fresh or
butterfish	mussels	canned)
carp (fresh)	oysters	weakfish
clams	pike	whiting
crab	porgy	GROUP B
croaker	salmon (canned)	mackerel
cod	scallops	pompano
finnan haddie	shad roe	salmon (fresh)
flounder	shrimp	shad
fluke	sole	white fish

Add 2 ounces to raw fish weight to allow for loss in cooking.
Add 2 ounces for fish with bones.

BASTES (to use on fish while it is broiling or baking)

* Tomato juice (plain or with added herbs)
  Clam juice
  Vegetable stock
  Chicken consommé
* Skim milk
* Creole sauce
  Celery sauce

  BBQ Baste
  Worcestershire sauce diluted with water
  Lemon juice
  Lemon juice and chopped parsley
  Soy sauce

BROILING FISH STEAKS

Cod, salmon, swordfish, fresh tuna, halibut, striped bass, are only a few of the fish which you can buy cut into steaks. Broil fresh steaks about 1 inch from heat, 3-5 minutes on each side. Baste them at least once while they are broiling. (Thin steaks do not require turning.)

BROILING WHOLE DRESSED FISH

Broil bluefish, butterfish, flounder, fluke, and porgy 3 inches from heat, allowing a total of 8-10 minutes. Broil flounder and fluke white side up without turning. The other fish should be turned once.

Broil the heavier whole fish such as carp, croaker, mackerel, mullet, pike, weakfish, whitefish and whiting 6 inches from heat. Allow 5-8 minutes on each side, turning once (allow 13 minutes on each side for carp).

Baste fish at least once while broiling using any of the recommended bastes.

BROILING SPLIT FISH

Split fish should be broiled about 3 inches from heat, allowing a total broiling time of 6-12 minutes. Do not overcook; fish should flake easily when done without being dry. Baste at least once.

BROILING FISH FILLETS

Fresh fillets should be set about ½ inch from heat, for a total broiling time of 5-8 minutes, basting once. Fillets of bluefish, carp, cod, flounder, fluke, haddock, hake, mackerel, mullet, pike, porgy, sea bass, sole, weakfish, whitefish and whiting are all available at some time. Baste them at least once. Do not overcook. Broil only one side.

Frozen fish fillets can be broiled without being defrosted, but allow a few minutes longer. Baste at least once.

BUYING FISH

Light-red gills denote freshness, dark red, staleness. Eyes should be bright, not sunken. Scales should cling to skin. The odor should be good.

"BREADED" FISH

Fish fillets and steaks may be wiped with paper towels, dipped in water or brushed with lemon juice, then sprinkled with *non-fat dry milk solids or (for luncheon only) dipped into *bread crumbs, before they are baked or broiled. The bread crumbs can be made from crusts of luncheon bread whizzed up in the blender. Season the crumbs with salt, pepper, rosemary, etc.

Prepare special sauce, spread on Cod and bake until done. Who said diets can't be fun?

* Limited food—see Menu Plan, p. 18-20, for legal amount.

FISH STOCK

(To be used in making fish soups, stews, chowders and sauces)

> 2 or 3 pounds fish trimmings (bones and head
>   of fish)
> 1 cup mixed diced celery and dehydrated onion
>   flakes
> 2 cloves
> 4 peppercorns
> 1 small bay leaf
> 2 sprigs parsley
> 1 sprig thyme
> 1 teaspoon salt
> 2 quarts cold water

Bring to boiling point in large kettle, skim and cook together gently for about 2 hours. Strain and use as stock for broiling or poaching fish or as base for soup.

Fish cooked in stock is much more delicious than when water alone is used. Use stock also as the base for bouillabaisse or any fish preparation. Ask the fish man for the trimmings. Escarole or Cantonese Soup are also delicious when made from fish stock.

STRIPED BASS ROSEMARY

> *1 four-pound striped bass
> Salt and freshly ground black pepper to taste
> 1 teaspoon chopped rosemary
> ½ cup fish or chicken stock
> 1 tablespoon wine vinegar

Preheat oven to 400°F. Have fish cleaned and scaled, but leave head and tail intact. Weigh it, allowing 12 ounces for men, 10 ounces for women at dinner. Rinse the fish under cold water and pat dry with paper towels. Sprinkle inside and out with salt and pepper. Place in a baking dish and sprinkle rosemary around it. Bake the fish, basting with stock every three minutes or so. When fish flakes easily when tested with a fork, transfer to a hot serving platter. Add the vinegar to the baking dish, heat thoroughly and pour pan drippings over the fish. Garnish with lemon slices.

CLAM JUICE

You can buy clam juice bottled or canned. Great to use as stock for poaching fish. Try it mixed with *tomato juice as a baste for fish.

CLAM BISQUE

Liquid from canned clams (about ½ cup)
*2 cups skim milk
½ teaspoon Worcestershire sauce
Grated nutmeg
Salt and pepper to taste
*8-ounce can of minced clams packed in their own
    liquid (4 ounces of clams)
Paprika

Combine liquid from canned clams with skim milk and bring to boiling point. Add Worcestershire sauce and a slight grating of nutmeg. Taste and add salt and pepper if desired. Serve over clams in bowl with sprinkling of paprika. Two luncheon servings, 2 ounces each.

The bisque may be made considerably richer by the addition of *nonfat dry milk solids. Count added powder toward day's skim milk allowance: ⅓ cup powder equals 1 glass skim milk.

QUICK MANHATTAN CLAM CHOWDER

   *¾ cup tomato juice
   ¾ cup chicken stock (may be made from instant
      chicken broth mix)
   *1 can (8 ounces) minced clams
   ½ cup juice from clams
   Pinch of thyme
   Suggestion of red hot pepper

Combine liquids, bring to boil, add thyme and pepper if you are
using it. Cook 3 minutes. Meanwhile divide minced clams into two
chowder mugs. Pour hot soup into mugs and serve immediately.
Clams will be juicy and tender if they are not cooked. 2 servings.
Count each serving as 2 ounces of fish. (Note: Clams packed with
liquid will weigh about 4 ounces net.)

MANHATTAN CLAM CHOWDER

Follow recipe above but dice celery, dehydrated reconstituted onion
and green pepper (in small even squares) and cook separately in
chicken stock. Add to soup before pouring into bowls holding
*clams.

STUFFED CLAMS

   *2 dozen large clams
   ¼ cup water
   ½ cup chopped mushrooms
   Sautéed onion powder
   Chopped parsley
   *Tomato juice
   Salt
   Pepper
   Oregano

Wash and scrub clams. Place in kettle with seasoned water (salt, pepper, parsley, oregano). Bring to a boil. Steam until clams open. Remove clams from shells. Weigh allowed portion. Save half the shells. Chop clams very fine. Mix with mushrooms that have been sautéed in a non-stick pan. Mix clams with all other ingredients. Place mixture in clam shells. Bake in 400°F. oven for 5 minutes.

COD FISH AU PLAT

Parsley
6 mushrooms
1 tablespoon dehydrated onion flakes soaked in
  water
1 bay leaf
1 pinch thyme
Salt and pepper
½ cup fish stock, chicken stock or water
2 pimentos
*1 pound cod fillet

Mince parsley and mushrooms. Put in saucepan with onion flakes (save water), bay leaf and thyme. Sprinkle with salt and pepper. Add fish stock, chicken stock or water and the water in which onion flakes were soaked. Cover and cook ½ hour. Remove to blender and beat with pimentos. Cook again until reduced to half. Spread sauce on fish in a shallow baking dish, and bake uncovered for 15 minutes at 375°F. or until fish is done.

CURRY OF COD

1 pound cod fillet
1 tablespoon curry powder
*3 tablespoons nonfat dry milk
½ cup fish stock, chicken stock or clam juice

Cut cod fillet into long strips. Heat curry powder, milk and fish stock or chicken stock. Add cod and cook until done. Serve with chopped parsley. Use weighed portion at luncheon or dinner.

COD BAKE

    *2 pounds cod, fresh or frozen
     ¼ cup dehydrated onion flakes
     1 clove garlic, minced
     ¼ cup chicken or fish stock
    *3 medium-sized apples, pared, quartered cored
       and sliced
    *6 ounces tomato sauce (12 ounces tomato juice,
       cooked to half its volume)
     ¾ cup water
     2 teaspoons salt
     ⅛ teaspoon pepper

Have cod cut into weighed portions for 6. Place in a shallow baking dish. Cook onion flakes and garlic in chicken or fish stock in saucepan until soft; stir in remaining ingredients. Heat, stirring constantly, to boiling; spoon over fish; cover. Bake in moderate oven (350°F.) about 45 minutes, or until fish flakes easily. 6 servings; count ½ fruit for each.

BAKED FISH STEAK

Sprinkle weighed *fish steak with lemon juice, salt and pepper and bake in shallow pan in hot oven 425-450°F. until tender. A layer of partly cooked fresh vegetables—green beans, diced pepper, celery, mushrooms, bean sprouts, etc.—can be put into pan first, fish steak on top, and highly seasoned *Tomato Sauce W.W. poured over everything before baking.

CRAB MEAT SALAD

> *6 ounces clean crab meat, picked over to remove
>   bones, shell, etc.
> 1 tablespoon horseradish
> ¼ cup Tomato French Dressing W.W. (see index
>   for recipe)
> 2 tablespoons chopped green pepper
> 2 tablespoons chopped pickle
> 1 tablespoon chopped scallion
> 1 tablespoon lemon juice
> *Sour Cream W.W. (made from ⅓ cup cottage
>   cheese and water, liquefied in blender)
> Salt and pepper to taste

Put crab meat on cold platter. Combine other ingredients. Pour over crab. Serves 2 at luncheon.

QUICK CIOPPINO

This fish stew (pronounced choe-*peen*-o) is a California favorite, which, like bouillabaisse is prepared in many different versions. Crabs, clams, and a variety of fish and shellfish may be used. Here is a simple version.

> *1 onion, finely minced
> Chicken or fish stock, consommé, or water
> Chopped parsley
> 1 clove garlic, pressed or mashed
> *3 tomatoes, chopped
> *2 pounds firm solid fish such as striped bass or
>   rock cod
> Salt and pepper

* *All shellfish are in Group A (lean fish).*

Brown onion in hot dry skillet without added fat. As soon as it begins to color add a few tablespoons of chicken or fish stock, consommé or water to prevent onions from scorching. Add parsley and garlic and let cook 5 minutes. Add the tomatoes and mix to combine all ingredients. Now add the weighed fish and gently stir. Season to taste with salt and pepper and cook over moderate heat for about 20 minutes. Do not stir. Serves 4 at dinner and includes a limited vegetable. May be refrigerated and used for two days, 2 servings each.

CRAB CIOPPINO

Use equal amounts of uncooked *crab and *fish. Or combine equal amounts of crab, uncooked shelled *shrimp and fish. Washed *clams in the shell may also be added. Optional seasonings include basil, bay leaf, pepper, celery, and dried mushrooms. These may be added to the sauce before fish is put in.

CREOLE-STYLE BAKED FISH

> *2 cups tomato juice
> 2 cucumbers, finely diced
> 1 green pepper, finely diced
> 2 tablespoons dehydrated onion flakes, soaked in
>   water
> 1 cup celery, finely diced
> 1 garlic clove
> 2 cups water
> 1 teaspoon salt
> ½ teaspoon pepper

Put all ingredients into a kettle. Bring to boil. Let simmer 45 minutes. Store in refrigerator and use as a topping or a bed before baking fish. Unlimited, but watch count on tomato juice.

* Limited food—see Menu Plan, p. 18-20, for legal amount.

BAKED FISH FILLETS AU GRATIN

*1 pound fresh or frozen fish fillets, cut into 4
   servings
Salt and pepper
2 tablespoons lemon juice
½ cup Mushroom Sauce (see index for recipe)
*2 ounces grated sharp cheese
¼ teaspoon salt
⅛ teaspoon pepper

Arrange fish in shallow baking dish. Sprinkle lightly with salt,
pepper, and lemon juice. Cover with Mushroom Sauce; sprinkle
with cheese and paprika. Bake at 375°F. for about 15 minutes. 4
servings for luncheon.

FLOUNDER BIRD

1 flounder fillet (4 ounces after cooking)
2 teaspoons dehydrated onion flakes, soaked in fish
   stock, clam juice or water
2 tablespoons celery
*½ cup soft bread crumbs (made from 1 slice of
   allowed bread, cut into large pieces)

Wipe the flounder fillet with a damp cloth. Mince onion and celery
and combine with bread crumbs; moisten with liquid in which the
onion flakes were soaked. Use as filling for flounder. Broil or bake
quickly and serve at once for luncheon. 1 serving. Good with Sauce
Chambord.

   Note: Same recipe may be used for haddock.

*The fat content of fish varies according to species and season. Lean
fish, Group A, are best broiled; fat fish, Group B, baked.*

FILLET OF FLOUNDER MARGUERITE

  *5-ounce flounder fillet
  ¼ cup water
  ½ teaspoon lemon juice
  *3 tablespoons skim milk
  *3 ounces shrimp, scallops and canned clams,
     cut up
  2 mushrooms cut up
  ⅛ teaspoon salt
  Freshly grated pepper
  Nutmeg
  Dash paprika

Wipe fillet with moist paper towel and roll up. Pour water and lemon juice into skillet and bring to a simmer. Place fillet seamside down in the simmering water, cover and let fish poach for 2-3 minutes until it loses its transparent look. Remove to a shallow flameproof serving dish. Add skim milk to liquid in skillet and let simmer uncovered until liquid boils down about half. Add shrimps, scallops, clams and mushrooms and heat gently about 2 minutes. Stir in salt, pepper, nutmeg and dash of paprika. Put over fillet in broiling pan and brown high under broiler for 1 minute. One dinner serving.

ALL-IN-ONE BAKED FISH DINNER

  *8 ounces fish fillet (haddock or flounder)
  ½ teaspoon salt
  ¼ teaspoon pepper
  1 teaspoon onion powder
  *¼ cup tomato juice
  *½ cup frozen peas and carrots
  1 envelope vegetable bouillon mix

Wipe fish with damp towel. Place it in covered casserole or use baking dish with tin foil cover. Season with salt, pepper and onion.

Pour tomato juice and drained vegetables over fish. Bake in 400°F. preheated oven until fish becomes flaky. One serving; can easily be multiplied for family-size service. Note: Peas and carrots are a limited vegetable; measure portion.

BOILED FISH IN PAPER

4 pieces aluminum foil, 12 inches square
*4 boneless fillets, 8 ounces each
2 tablespoons coarse salt
1 cup water
¼ teaspoon pepper
¼ cup grated pimento
2 tablespoons dehydrated onion flakes
1 tablespoon chopped parsley
1 tablespoon lemon juice

Let fish stand in salt solution for 5 minutes, not longer. Put each fillet on aluminum foil. Combine remaining ingredients and divide over fish. Bring edges of foil together and twist to make bag. Place in kettle of boiling water and boil for 20 minutes. Four dinner servings. (This recipe can easily be reduced to serve 1.)

FAMILY FISH LOAF

*20 ounces cooked or canned flaked fish
*2 eggs, beaten
*1 cup Tomato Sauce W.W. (see index for recipe)
2 teaspoons dehydrated onion flakes, soaked in
    clam juice, fish stock or water
*½ cup fine bread crumbs (made in blender from
    1 slice of allowed bread)

Combine all ingredients, shape into loaf and bake in moderate oven for 30 minutes. Cover with *Creole Sauce for last 10 minutes.

Serves 3 women or teenagers, and 1 man. Good for Saturday or Sunday luncheon. (Includes eggs and cannot be used at dinner.)

BOUILLABAISSE

  1 quart fish stock or water
  3 tablespoons dehydrated onion
  3 cloves garlic, minced
 *6 ounces minced clams (save liquid)
 *8 ounces tomato juice
  2 teaspoons soy sauce
  1 teaspoon thyme, crumbled
  ½ teaspoon bottled dried orange peel or grated
     fresh rind of half an orange
  1 bay leaf, crumbled
  2 tablespoons minced parsley
  1½ teaspoons salt
  ½ teaspoon pepper
  1 package sugar substitute
 *2 pounds firm-fleshed fish steaks (snapper, bass,
     cod, haddock, perch, in any desired proportion
     but use exact legal weight)
  2 cups French-style green beans
 *1 pound lobster tail, cut in pieces
 *8 ounces raw shrimp, shelled and deveined

In large heavy kettle, boil fish stock or water, covered, with onion, garlic, clam juice, tomato juice and spices and seasonings for 1 hour. Add 2 pounds fish and green beans; boil hard for 5 minutes. Turn fire lower and drop in lobster and shrimp. Cook until shrimp are pink, about 5 minutes. Add clams just long enough to heat but not boil. Serve fish and broth in large soup bowls. Makes 8 servings and is a wonderful company dinner dish to serve with a tossed green salad.

Note: Add 2 ounces fish for each man.

* *Limited food—see Menu Plan, p. 18-20, for legal amount.*

HALIBUT BROIL

    3 tablespoons soy sauce
    1 teaspoon salt
    Pepper
    Garlic powder
    Lemon juice
    1 teaspoon dehydrated onion flakes
    1 teaspoon water
    *1 halibut steak (allowed serving for 1)
    Paprika

Prepare sauce by combining first 7 ingredients. Spread on both sides of fish. Sprinkle with paprika. Broil ¾ inch from heat for 8 minutes or until brown. Turn and brown second side if steak is thick.

PICKLED FISH

    ¼ cup dehydrated onion flakes soaked in water
        to cover
    *8 ounces fillet of pike
    Salt and pepper
    Liquid sugar substitute
    Lemon juice
    Pickling spices

Combine all ingredients and simmer with just enough water to cover for 30 minutes. Remove fish, strain liquid, pour over fish, and chill. 1 serving at dinner.

Frozen fish, if properly handled, will remain in perfect condition for months. Frozen fish fillets may be cooked without defrosting; follow package directions for thick slices.

    * *Limited food—see Menu Plan, p. 18-20, for legal amount.*

OCEAN PERCH SALAD

*4 ounces cooked ocean perch
4 tablespoons chopped celery
2 tablespoons Chambord Sauce (see index for
  recipe)
1 teaspoon chopped sweet pickle
1 teaspoon chopped green pepper
1 teaspoon chopped pimento

Combine all ingredients and serve as luncheon salad, with salad greens, cucumber slices, and a sprinkling of finely chopped dill leaves or chives. One luncheon serving.

MARINATED FISH

*4 onions, sliced
*6 slices fish (2 pounds), white fish, pike or
  haddock (weigh portions)
2 teaspoons salt
Black pepper
2 cups water
1½ cups white vinegar
1 tablespoon sugar substitute
2 teaspoons pickling spice
2 bay leaves

Combine 2 onions with the fish, salt, pepper and water in saucepan. Bring to a boil. Cover and cook over low heat for 35 minutes. Arrange fish in glass bowl or jar with remaining onions in layers. Add the vinegar, sugar substitute, pickling spice and bay leaves to stock. Bring to a boil and pour over fish. Let marinate for 3 days. This will jell and keep for 2 weeks.

EASY BAKED FISH WITH TOMATO SAUCE FOR ONE

> *1 portion haddock, halibut, flounder, whitefish, etc.
> *½ cup tomato juice
> 1 green pepper, chopped
> Sliced mushrooms
> Oregano
> Crushed bay leaf
> 1 or 2 stalks celery, sliced
> Salt and pepper to taste

Make a pan by folding heavy aluminum foil. Add fish. Pour all ingredients over fish and bake until tender in 375-400°F. oven. The easy part of the title refers to the clean-up.

ROLLED FILLETS OF FISH

> *Fillet of sole or flounder
> Salt and pepper
> Fish stock or clam juice
> Paprika
> *Tomato juice
> Pimento

Line custard cups with fillets. Season with salt and pepper. Partly fill cups with stock or clam juice and bake in 375°F. oven until fish is done, about 10 minutes. Put fillets on a plate and quickly boil up sauce with some paprika and tomato juice. Pour into center, garnish with strips of pimento and serve.

Object to fishy odor? Soak hands in cold water before handling fish. After handling, wash hands in hot water with salt (no soap until after you have rinsed off salt).

   * *Limited food—see Menu Plan, p. 18-20, for legal amount.*

FISH BAKED IN BUTTERMILK

    *2 portions haddock, halibut, flounder, fresh
      whitefish, etc.
    1 teaspoon dill
    1 teaspoon parsley
    ⅛ teaspoon dry mustard
    1 or 2 stalks celery, sliced
    Salt and pepper to taste
    Diced green pepper (if desired)
    *1 cup buttermilk or skimmed milk

Put the fish into a baking dish, add seasonings and pour milk over all. Bake until fish flakes easily (about ½ hour) in 375°F. oven.

MEDITERRANEAN BAKED HALIBUT

    *2 medium onions, thinly sliced
    1 clove garlic, crushed
    ½ cup parsley sprigs
    ½ teaspoon salt
    ⅛ teaspoon black pepper
    *1 cup Tomato Sauce W.W. (see index for recipe)
    2 chicken-bouillon cubes or envelopes chicken-broth mix
    *3 fresh halibut steaks (use exact weight allowed
      for dinner)
    *1 tomato, 3 thick slices
    3 thin lemon slices

Brown onions and garlic in a large skillet holding 3 tablespoons water. Add parsley, salt, pepper, Tomato Sauce, and bouillon cubes or broth mix. Simmer gently, uncovered, 20 minutes. Start heating oven to 350°F. Place fish steaks in 12x8x2-inch baking dish; cover with sauce, then top with tomato and lemon slices. Bake 20 to 25 minutes or until fish flakes easily. Makes 3 servings, and includes limited vegetable.

BAKED FLOUNDER FILLET LUNCHEON

*4 flounder fillets (3 ounces each)
  Seasoned salt
*4 slices Swiss cheese (totaling 2 ounces)
  ¼ teaspoon dehydrated onion
  1 small can mushrooms (reserve liquid) or ½ cup
    fresh
  2 teaspoons parsley (if desired)
*¼ cup skim milk
*¼ cup Tomato Sauce (see index for recipe)

Sprinkle fillets lightly on both sides with seasoned salt, then roll up each. Fold cheese in half. Arrange flounder rolls and cheese slices alternately down center of baking dish. Start heating oven to 400°F. Soak onion flakes in a few tablespoons hot fish stock or water till soft. Add mushrooms, ¾ teaspoon seasoned salt, parsley if used and mushroom liquid (with enough water added to make ¼ cup) or ¼ cup water if fresh mushrooms are used. Add skim milk and Tomato Sauce. Bring to boil and pour over fish. Bake 12 minutes or until fillets are golden and easily flaked with fork, but still moist. 4 servings.

QUICK STUFFED FISH

Ever try stuffing *fish fillets with chopped parsley and dill mixed with a crushed clove of garlic and moistened with lemon juice? Roll, and bake or broil. It's good. But the fish is limited, of course, so check weight.

ROMANIAN FISH GHIVETCH

Follow the directions for Vegetable Ghivetch (see index for recipe) but use a deeper casserole. Lay the *fish of your choice, washed but

* *Limited food—see Menu Plan, p. 18-20, for legal amount.*

still whole, on top of vegetables. Cook, covered, in moderate oven until vegetables are almost soft. About 20 minutes before they are done, uncover pan and raise heat to brown top. The vegetables are unlimited; weigh the fish as required.

FISH AND APPLES

Slice *4 apples ¼-inch thick. Cook gently in a shallow pan (that can be put under broiler) in a few tablespoons of water, salt and ¼ teaspoon sugar substitute. When almost tender, put 2 pounds fish fillets on the apples, cover and allow to steam 5 minutes. Remove cover and turn fish, season with salt and pepper and put under broiler until well browned. Weigh fish; count apples.

FISH SOUFFLE WITH VEGETABLE SAUCE

    *14 ounces any cooked fish (halibut and cod are
       good)
    *1 cup heated (but not boiled) skim milk
     2 teaspoons grated onion for flavor
    *1 egg, separated
    *½ cup bread crumbs (1 slice bread whirred in
       blender)

Mash fish with onion, egg yolk and bread crumbs. Stir in milk, then fold in stiffly beaten whites. Put into casserole, set in pan of water and bake 40 minutes at 300°F. Soufflé will rise and top will brown. Serves 4 at lunch.

VEGETABLE SAUCE

Slice ¼ pound mushrooms, 1 small green pepper and 1 stalk celery. Cook in saucepan with *1 cup tomato juice until vegetables are soft and liquid is reduced to about half. Add 1 cup cooked young green beans and serve hot over soufflé.

LOBSTER TAILS—BROIL OR BOIL?

It's up to you. Either way, they're simply delicious—and a snap to prepare (which might surprise you). Let us prove it to you here and now!

HOW TO BOIL LOBSTER TAILS

Drop frozen rock-lobster tails into boiling salted water to cover. When water boils again, simmer 3 minutes longer than approximate weight of 1 tail (9 minutes for a 6-ounce tail). Drain and weigh cooked lobster tails. With scissors, cut away thin underside membrane —cut down each side and remove under shell, or make 1 bold cut through center and spread to expose meat. To remove lobster meat, grasp tail securely. Insert your index finger between shell and meat; pull firmly. Chill lobster; then flake or cube for your favorite salad or sauce.

HOW TO BROIL LOBSTER TAILS

With a sharp knife, cut down through center of hard top shell of frozen tail; cut through meat, but not through under shell. Spread open, butterfly-style, so meat is on top. Place tails on broiler rack, shell side down. Dash few drops of bottled hot pepper sauce into Tomato French Dressing W.W.; brush over lobster meat. Broil 4 to 5 inches from heat or 8 to 10 minutes. Avoid overcooking. Meat is done when it can be flaked with a fork. To serve—loosen meat by inserting fork between shell and meat.

LOBSTER AND PINEAPPLE KABOBS

Place a bright-red *lobster in center of a large oval platter. Arrange kabobs of chunks of fresh *pineapple (from which core has been removed) and chunks of weighed cooked *lobster meat (lobster tails are good for this) Serve with bowl of Tomato French Dressing, Celery Sauce or Chambord Sauce. Check weight of fish and count fruit before preparing so you do not exceed allowance. Good when you are entertaining.

BROILED SEAFOOD CAKES

> *12 ounces finely chopped cooked shrimp, lobster
>   or crab meat
> 2 tablespoons chopped parsley
> 1 tablespoon chopped fresh dill or dried dill seeds
> ¼ teaspoon curry (optional)
> Salt and pepper to taste
> *2 eggs
> *Buttermilk

Mix sea food with herbs and seasonings. Break in eggs. Mix vigorously. Add enough buttermilk to allow for shaping the mixtures into cakes. Should have 4-6 cakes, depending on size desired. Broil on both sides until well browned. Yield: 4 luncheon servings; the shellfish are 3 servings; the eggs, 1.

Going on vacation?
Pack your suitcase...
not your stomach!

SEA FOOD EN COQUILLE

*1 egg
*10 ounces chopped boiled shrimp, lobster or
    crab meat
 1 tablespoon chopped parsley
*1 tablespoon tomato juice
 1 tablespoon horseradish
 Salt and pepper
 ½ teaspoon lemon juice
*1 tablespoon dry skim milk
*¼ cup bread crumbs (from 1 slice bread
    crumbled in blender)

Beat egg and combine with other ingredients, except milk powder
and bread crumbs. Mix lightly with fork and fill 3 shells or custard
cups or a casserole. Sprinkle skim milk over each shell, top with
crumbs and bake at 375°F. until brown. Three luncheon portions.

SALMON OR TUNA BAKE

    *1 slice bread
    Celery
    Green pepper
    1 teaspoon onion flakes
    Lemon juice
    *1 egg
    *6 ounces canned salmon or tuna, drained

Put bread into blender to make crumbs and remove. Then put vegetables into blender and blend until puréed. Combine crumbs, puréed vegetables, lemon juice, egg and fish. Turn into baking pan. Bake in oven at 375°F. for 15 minutes. Two luncheon servings.

SALMON AND FLOUNDER ROLL

Have the obliging fish dealer roll a small fillet of *flounder around a small piece of *salmon. Keep in place with toothpicks. It looks like a bagel. Season with salt, pepper and lemon juice. Bake or broil for 20 minutes in moderate oven, 350°F. Flounder and salmon combined must not exceed legal weight.

SALMON PATTY

    *2 ounces canned salmon, drained
    *Crust of luncheon toast (crumbled)
    *1 egg
    ⅛ teaspoon salt
    Dash Worcestershire sauce
    Pinch pepper
    1 teaspoon onion juice

To salmon add the crumbled crust of your luncheon toast. Add remaining ingredients and mix very well. Fry in Teflon pan or broil on slow fire. Serve with slices of dilled cucumbers. One serving.

SALMON-STUFFED CHILI PEPPERS

4 medium green peppers
½ teaspoon salt
1 tablespoon dehydrated onion flakes
3 tablespoons minced celery
Few tablespoons water or stock
*1 cup fresh bread crumbs (2 slices bread crumbled
    in blender)
*6 ounces canned salmon, drained
½ teaspoon salt
¼ teaspoon pepper
¼ teaspoon oregano
1 teaspoon chili powder
*1 egg, beaten

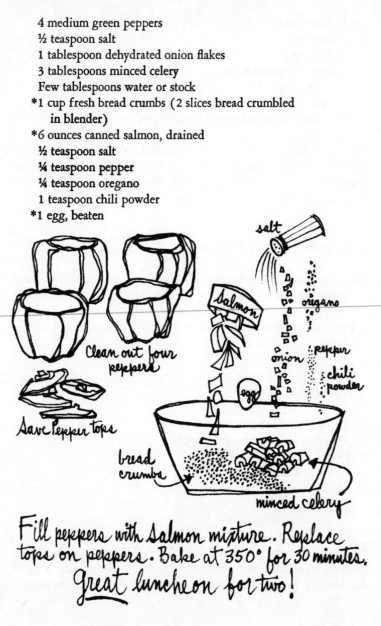

Clean out four peppers

Save Pepper tops

salt

salmon

oregano

onion

pepper

chili powder

egg

bread crumbs

minced celery

Fill peppers with Salmon mixture. Replace tops on peppers. Bake at 350° for 30 minutes.

Great luncheon for two!

Cut a thin slice from top of green peppers and scoop out seeds and membranes. Trim stems from tops. Parboil peppers and tops in boiling water to cover with ½ teaspoon salt for 5 minutes. Drain and cool. Place peppers close together in baking dish. Cook onion and celery in a few tablespoons water or stock for 3 minutes or until soft. In a bowl combine bread crumbs, drained salmon, salt, pepper, oregano, chili, egg, cooked onion and celery. Mix lightly. Spoon into green peppers. Place trimmed tops on top of peppers and bake in 350°F. oven for 30 minutes. Garnish with parsley. Good luncheon dish for 2; it is easily reheated.

DEVILED SALMON

   *2 cups tomato juice, cooked down to 1 cup
      tomato sauce
   3 teaspoons dehydrated onion flakes
   ¼ green pepper
   ½ teaspoon salt
   ½ teaspoon prepared mustard
   *1 pound canned drained salmon
   6 thin slices lemon, including peel
   *¼ cup fine crumbs (½ slice bread made into
      crumbs in blender)

Blend first 5 ingredients for about 15 seconds. Flake salmon. Combine with sauce from blender and turn into casserole. Top with crumbs, then with lemon slices. Bake at 400°F. for 25 minutes. Serves 4 at luncheon. This recipe is easily reduced to serve 1 or 2; or it may be prepared for 4 and frozen in single portions.

CASSEROLE LUNCHEON FOR FOUR

Herbal Asparagus Soup, p. 149
Deviled Salmon
Fresh Fruit Salad, p. 242

SALMON OR TUNA PUFF

> *8 ounces salmon or tuna, drained
> *1 cup skim milk
> ½ cup mushrooms, cut into slices through cap
>   and stem
> ¼ cup chopped green pepper or pimento
> Salt and pepper
> *2 eggs, separated

Combine salmon or tuna, skim milk, mushrooms, green pepper or pimento in shallow baking dish. Season with salt and pepper, and heat in moderate oven (375°F.). Meanwhile beat egg whites with a dash of salt until stiff. Beat egg yolks. Fold egg whites into yolks, a little at a time, pour over hot fish and put back into oven for another 20 minutes. Serve hot. Tops will be brown and puffy. Three servings at luncheon.

SCALLOPS EN BROCHETTE

Impale a portion of *scallops on steel skewers alternating with squares of red pimento or slices of mushroom. Impale the skewers so they slant upright, in a squash, block of wood, or even a clean flower-arranging pin holder. Bake until scallops are opaque white.

MARINATED SCALLOPS AND APPLES

Marinate small *scallops in Tomato French Dressing W.W. (see index for recipe page). String on skewers alternating with unpeeled *apple. Broil until golden brown. Weigh scallops and count fruit.

* *Limited food—see Menu Plan, p. 18-20, for legal amount.*

SEA FOOD DELAWARE

    3 teaspoons dehydrated onion
    2 green peppers, chopped
    1 clove garlic (or powder)
    A little paprika
    ½ teaspoon salt
    A little pepper
  *2 tomatoes, cut up
  *1 pound uncooked shrimp or lobster (raw cleaned
       weight)
    Sugar substitute to taste

Cook onion, green pepper, garlic, paprika, salt, pepper and tomatoes for 10 minutes or until peppers are tender. Add shrimp or lobster. Add sugar substitute to sweeten. Cover and simmer 10 minutes more. Two servings; include limited vegetable.

SEA FOOD CASSEROLE

    1 cup chopped celery
    1 roast pimento
    2 teaspoons dehydrated onion flakes
    Few tablespoons fish stock or water
    Ground ginger
  *3 ounces canned crab meat, flaked
  *3 ounces cooked, shelled shrimp
    ½ cup Tomato French Dressing W.W.

Cook celery, pimento and dehydrated onion in a few tablespoons fish stock or water. When most of liquid has boiled away and vegetables are soft, season with ground ginger. Arrange in a small casserole: a layer of vegetables, a layer of crab meat, a layer of vegetables, and a layer of shrimp. Top with Tomato French Dressing. Bake in moderate oven (350°F.) for half an hour.

BROILED SHAD ROE

Try the canned *shad roe, brown it on both sides under the broiler, then serve with a lemon juice and parsley sauce (see index).

TIPS ON COOKING SHRIMP

To cook *1 pound of shrimp, use a covered saucepan. Prepare a stock of 1 cup water, 1 teaspoon salt, and ½ stalk of celery. Simmer the stock and when it has reached the boiling point, lower the heat, add the shrimp and let simmer for no more than 5 minutes. The shrimp *should not be allowed to boil*—keep them at simmering temperature only.

You can cut down the cooking odor if you will shell the shrimp before cooking. The simple tools which shell and devein shrimp at the same time are a great help.

STORING SHRIMP

Keep fresh shrimp tightly wrapped in the refrigerator until ready to cook. After cooking, refrigerate shrimps in a tightly covered container in the stock in which they were cooked. This will keep them juicy.

BUTTERFLY SHRIMP SCAMPI

> *Shrimp—2 dinner portions
> Artificial butter flavor
> 4 teaspoons dehydrated onion flakes
> Garlic powder
> Parsley flakes (or fresh parsley finely minced)
> Chives
> Paprika
> Juice of 2 lemons

Leave the tail on the shrimp. Split each shrimp lengthwise with a sharp knife down to the tail, but leave tail intact. Lay them in a shallow baking pan in rows, head to tail. Dot each shrimp with artificial butter flavor; soak onion flakes in water, then chop and sprinkle over shrimp, including liquid in which onion soaked. Now sprinkle generously with garlic powder, parsley, chives and paprika. At last sprinkle with juice of two lemons. Let shrimp marinate for an hour or so. Then put the pan under the broiler (4 inches from heat) and cook about 15 minutes or until tails begin to char and shrimps are done. Serve shrimp with juices poured over them. Serves 2 at dinner. (Allowed shrimp weight, including tail, is 8 ounces after cooking for women; 10 ounces for men. Add 2 ounces to get weight before cooking.)

SHRIMP SCAMPI

¼ cup chicken stock or water
*½ large onion or 6 shallots
1 large clove garlic, minced
2 teaspoons minced parsley
Dash oregano
*Prawn or colossal shrimp, cleaned

In a heavy saucepan holding stock or water, steam all ingredients except shrimp for 10 minutes. Bake shrimp in 350°F. oven for 25 minutes. Add sauce and brown in broiler 5 minutes. (Watch weight of shrimp—do not exceed allowed amount.)

POLYNESIAN SHRIMP

1 medium green pepper, cut into 1-inch pieces
2 tablespoons fish stock or water
*½ cup unsweetened pineapple juice
2 teaspoons lemon juice
1 tablespoon soy sauce
*½ cup pineapple chunks
*1½ cups cooked shrimp (or 4 allowed portions)

In skillet, cook green pepper in stock or water until tender. Remove from heat; add fruit juices, soy sauce and pineapple. Cook until thickened; stir constantly. Add shrimps. Heat. 4 servings. Serve on your prettiest platter. It's exciting enough for a company meal!

CHINESE SHRIMP WITH BEAN SPROUTS

>   1 pound bean sprouts
>   1 clove garlic
>   1 teaspoon ginger root
> *1 pound uncooked shrimp, washed, shelled and
>   deveined
>   ¼ cup chicken stock or water
>   3 tablespoons soy sauce
>   1 tablespoon chives, finely diced

Wash bean sprouts in a large bowl of water. Remove with slotted spoon and set aside. Put garlic, ginger root, and shrimp in preheated heavy 10-inch pan and cook and stir for 4 minutes. Remove garlic. Add chicken stock or water and soy sauce. Cover pan and cook 3 minutes. Add drained sprouts. Cover pan and cook 3 minutes more. Sprinkle chives over shrimp. Serves 2 at dinner.

SHRIMP CHOP SUEY

> *1 pound raw shrimp (should be about 8 ounces
>   when shelled and cleaned)
> *1 tomato
>   ½ cup Chinese cabbage, cut up
>   4 large celery sticks cut in squares (use generously)
>   ½ chopped green pepper
>   2 cups bean sprouts (use generously)
>   Soy sauce

Clean shrimp, removing shells and veins. Slice them thin. Brown
in a hot dry skillet or non-stick pan. Add tomato, cabbage, celery,
green pepper and very little water. Cook until vegetables are done.
Parboil bean sprouts in separate pan and add these last. Season with
soy sauce. Serves 1 at dinner and includes limited vegetable.

ORIENTAL SHRIMP AND FISH

   *1 pound fillet of flounder, pike or haddock
   *1 pound fresh uncooked shrimp, shelled, cleaned
        and deveined (will be 8 ounces when cooked
        and cleaned)
    1 teaspoon salt
    Dash pepper
    1 tablespoon soy sauce
    3 tablespoons chicken stock
   *2 tablespoons finely minced scallion

Put flounder and shrimp through food chopper and place in baking
dish. Add remaining ingredients and mix well. Set baking dish in a
pan holding hot water, cover baking dish and cook about 30 minutes. Fish will be deliciously steamed. Serve with more soy sauce.

SHRIMP STEW LOUISIANA

    2 teaspoons dehydrated onion
    2 green peppers, cut up
    ½ cup hot water, fish stock or consommé
   *1 package frozen okra, sliced
   *2 tomatoes, cut up
   *1½ pounds cooked cleaned shrimp

Heat heavy skillet, add onion flakes and peppers and as soon as they
begin to brown add water, stock or consommé. Let cook until most
of liquid evaporates, and onions and peppers are soft. Add okra and

tomatoes and cook over gentle heat for 15 minutes, stirring occasionally to keep from burning. At the very last, add shrimp and let them heat but not boil. Serve in soup plates. Four dinner servings; includes limited vegetable.

Note: This dish may be divided into 4 individual casseroles and frozen. If used for a man's dinner, add 2 ounces (net cooked weight) of shrimp.

SHRIMP UNDER WRAPS

  *8 ounces cleaned and deveined shrimp
  1 tablespoon chopped scallion
  MSG
  8 thin slices green beans or cucumber or thin sticks
    celery
  ¼ teaspoon minced garlic
  ½ teaspoon salt
  *1 teaspoon tomato juice or water
  8 French-style green beans (uncooked)
  Aluminum foil

Put shrimp and other ingredients in the middle of a 12-inch square of aluminum foil. Wrap foil by bringing all sides together and pinching top. This will make a tight bag. Place in kettle with 1 inch boiling water, cover kettle and cook 15 minutes (or bake 15-20 minutes in 400°F. oven). Serve in foil. Serves 1 at dinner.

SWEET AND SOUR SHRIMP

  *2 ounces cooked cleaned shrimp, cut up
  *1 hard-cooked chopped egg
  4 tablespoons Chinese Sweet and Sour Sauce (see
    index for recipe)

Combine all ingredients in a small saucepan, heat gently and serve for luncheon over shredded Chinese cabbage or bean sprouts. One serving.

SHRIMP OR LOBSTER FLORIDA

Onion flakes
2 summer squash, sliced
1 clove garlic, minced
⅛ teaspoon paprika
½ teaspoon salt
½ cup diced peppers
⅛ teaspoon basil
¼ cup water
*4 tomatoes
*4 dinner portions fresh shrimp, or lobster,
    shelled and deveined

Cook onion flakes, squash, garlic, paprika, salt, pepper and basil in water. Cover and cook 10 minutes or until peppers are tender. Add the tomatoes, cover and cook five minutes. Blend in shrimp or lobster, cover and simmer (do not boil) a few minutes longer. Add water or tomato juice as necessary. Serve with green salad. Four dinner servings.

SHRIMP MOLD

1 tablespoon unflavored gelatin
*1 cup tomato juice
½ tablespoon lemon juice
1 tablespoon chopped pickle
*6 ounces cooked shrimp, cut in half (8 ounces for
    man's dinner)

Sprinkle gelatin over ¼ cup tomato juice. Heat remaining tomato juice. Add gelatin, lemon juice, pickle and shrimp. Put into wet mold and let set. Serves 1 at dinner.

SWORDFISH KABOBS

      *2 pounds swordfish (or 4 dinner portions)
      1 4-ounce can button mushrooms, drained
      2 tablespoons lemon juice
      ½ cup Tomato French Dressing W.W. (see index
         for recipe)

Cut fish into large chunks. Sprinkle with lemon juice. Marinate in Tomato French Dressing. String on skewers alternating with mushrooms and broil, turning once.

SWORDFISH DIABLO

      *2 swordfish steaks, 8 ounces each
      ½ teaspoon salt
      ¼ teaspoon pepper
      ½ teaspoon garlic powder
      ½ teaspoon onion powder
      ¼ cup prepared mustard

Ask a nice man at the fish store to divide the steaks into 8-ounce servings. If he's the man we think he is, he'll know you're on that Weight Watchers Program.

Wash fish steaks and pat dry. Sprinkle generously with salt, pepper, garlic powder and onion powder. Broil till flaky but not dry on hottest flame close to fire, 6 to 16 minutes depending on thickness of steak. Just before removing from fire spread thin layer of mustard over entire surface of fish. Broil. Serve at once. For man's dinner, increase weight of fish by two ounces.

MUSHROOMS STUFFED WITH TUNA—
A LUNCHEON SPECIAL

Prepare 12 large mushrooms for stuffing by removing stems and chopping them. Cook stems until soft with a tablespoon of chicken broth or water. Drain *4 ounces of tuna fish, flake fish, add mushroom stems, ½ teaspoon lemon juice, 1 tablespoon chopped dill weed or parsley and ⅛ teaspoon thyme. Mix well and season to taste with pepper. Pile caps with mixture. Make bread crumbs using *½ slice bread from luncheon allowance, put through blender or grinder. Sprinkle crumbs over mushroom caps. Put caps into a shallow baking dish and bake at 375°F. for 10 minutes or until well heated and lightly browned.

TUNA CHAMBORD

Heat Sauce Chambord with cut-up slivers of pimento. Add allowed tuna fish, well drained. Heat quickly without boiling and serve at once on toast.

SALAD NICOISE

       *8 ounces canned tuna, drained
       *1 cup Tomato French Dressing (see index)
        1 clove garlic, crushed
        1 teaspoon grated onion juice
        1 tablespoon chopped tarragon, 1¼ teaspoon if dried
        1 tablespoon chopped chives, 1¼ teaspoon if dried
        1 green pepper, cut in rings
        1 cup cooked string beans
        ½ cup cut pimento
        1 head lettuce, torn into pieces
       *4 hard-cooked eggs, cut in quarters

Combine first 10 ingredients and marinate until ready to serve. Just before serving toss over cut-up lettuce in salad bowl. Garnish with eggs. Serves 4.

TUNA CASSEROLE FLORENTINE MELANGE

Make a bed of chopped cooked spinach. Season with salt, freshly ground pepper and nutmeg. Top with weighed portion of flaked, drained canned *tuna fish. Mask it generously with Celery Sauce (see index for recipe), sprinkle with paprika, and pop into hot oven until brown and well heated, about half an hour.

So what if you're a perfect 20 .... wouldn't you rather be an imperfect 9 ?

TUNA WALDORF SALAD (FOR LUNCHEON)

* *1 red apple, unpeeled and diced
  1 tablespoon lemon juice (sprinkled on apple)
* *4 ounces canned tuna fish, drained and flaked
  1 tablespoon chopped pickle
  1 tablespoon chopped pimento
  ¼ cup chopped raw Chinese cabbage or cucumber

Chill and serve on bed of lettuce. Surround with the following (optional) additions of unlimited food: chopped cooked green beans, diced raw celery, diced radishes. Good with Chinese Sweet and Sour Sauce.

LOBSTER SALAD

Follow recipe but replace tuna fish with cut-up lobster.

CHEF'S SALAD LUNCHEON

  Lettuce
* *4 ounces drained tuna
  ½ jar (7½ ounces) sweet roasted peppers, cut up
  ½ cucumber, sliced
  2 tablespoons chopped celery
  1 tablespoon vinegar or lemon juice
  Salt and pepper
* *1 slice crisp toast

Shred lettuce in salad bowl. Arrange tuna, peppers, cucumber, and celery on lettuce. Sprinkle with vinegar or lemon juice and salt and pepper to taste. Serve with 1 slice crisp toast cut into 4 wedges or top with croutons you have made from white bread allowance. Add tomato juice, coffee or tea and a baked apple—I dare you to be hungry!

PUFFY TUNA SANDWICH

*6 ounces canned tuna, drained of all oil and flaked
2-3 tablespoons Chambord Sauce (see index for
    recipe)
*3 slices bread, lightly toasted
1 tablespoon tomato juice
*3 ounces hard cheese, shredded

Combine tuna and Chambord Sauce and mix well. Pile onto toast,
sprinkle with tomato juice and top with cheese. Broil 4 inches from
heat until puffy and brown, and cheese is melted. Serves 3 at
luncheon.

TURKISH FISH PILAKI (STEW)

*2 pounds bass, bluefish or swordfish
2 teaspoons dehydrated onion flakes
⅓ cup chopped parsley
1 clove garlic
*4 tomatoes
4 cups water
Salt and pepper

That obliging fish man will be glad to cut this fish into 4 legal
servings. Combine all ingredients in pot, cover and cook for 1 hour.
Serve hot or cold in soup bowls. Four servings which include limited
vegetable.

* Limited food—see Menu Plan, p. 18-20, for legal amount.

Meat and Poultry

RULES FOR USING MEAT AND POULTRY

Select a maximum of 5 weekly meat meals (luncheons or dinners) from the following:

GROUP A

white meat of chicken (skin removed)
white meat of turkey (skin removed)
pheasant
organ meats (liver, lungs, brains,
    kidneys, heart, sweetbreads)
rabbit
veal

Select a maximum of 3 weekly meat meals (luncheons or dinners) from the following:

GROUP B

beef
frankfurters
lamb
dark meat of turkey

For luncheon: 4 ounces boneless cooked meat or poultry may be
    selected, following Menu Plan.

For dinner: 6 ounces boneless cooked meat or poultry may be
    selected for women and teenagers, 8 ounces for men.

Add 2 ounces to get weight of uncooked meat; 2 ounces more if it
    has bone.

The recipes which follow give only the approximate weight of meat.
    Weigh your portion.

BROILED STEAK

No question about it—there are few things in life as popular as a
broiled *steak, cooked as you like it and for me that's on the rare
side and smothered in mushrooms. Of course, every bit of visible
fat must be cut off first, and if it is marbled with fat you can't cut

off, don't use the juice until you have chilled it, allowing the fat
to rise to the surface and be skimmed off. Weigh steak after cooking before serving at dinner: 6 ounces for women and teenagers;
8 ounces for men.

BEEF CHOP SUEY

> *2 pounds lean shoulder steak, cut into thin slices
> 1 cup sliced mushrooms
> 1 tablespoon dehydrated onion
> 1½ cups meat stock, or 1½ cups water with 2
>   bouillon cubes
> 1½ tablespoons soy sauce
> ⅛ teaspoon pepper
> 1 cup thinly sliced celery
> 2 green peppers sliced in thin rings

Brown meat, mushrooms and onions in broiler or in preheated heavy
iron skillet. Cook remaining ingredients in saucepan for 30 minutes.
Add browned meat. Cover and simmer for a few minutes or until
meat is tender. Serve with English mustard (made with dry mustard
mixed to paste with water). Serves 4.

CHINESE BEEF AND TURNIPS

> *2 pounds lean beef
> 1½ cups water
> 3 tablespoons soy sauce
> ½ teaspoon salt
> 3 slices ginger (or ground ginger)
> *2 cups yellow turnips

Wash beef and cut into 1-inch cubes. Put in heavy kettle with water
and bring quickly to boil, then add soy sauce, salt and ginger. Turn
heat down and let cook 1 hour. Cut turnips into wedges about
1½ inches big, add to meat and cook another hour.

CHINESE BEEF AND CABBAGE CASSEROLE

*1½ pounds (or three portions) sirloin steak,
    ¼-inch thick, cut in strips
½ cup soy sauce
1 teaspoon liquid sugar substitute
½ cup beef broth
1 cup sliced celery
*1 cup sliced bamboo shoots
½ pound thin sliced mushrooms (or 12 Chinese
    mushrooms, soaked in water for ½ hour)
*½ cup scallion, minced
1 small piece ginger, minced (or powdered ginger)
1 cup Chinese cabbage

Have pan very hot. Brown the meat quickly. Push it to one side. Combine soy sauce, liquid sugar substitute, and beef broth. Pour half the mixture over the meat. Cook the celery in the skillet for 3 minutes; push to one side again. Add remaining ingredients, cover pan and cook 15 minutes. Three servings, including limited vegetable.

BEEF AND EGGPLANT CASSEROLE

*1½ pounds lean beef, cut into ½-inch cubes
*1 eggplant, peeled and sliced
2 green peppers, diced
Onion powder or flakes for seasoning
Salt
Pepper
1 teaspoon oregano
*1 cup tomato juice
Water
*1 tomato, sliced (optional)

Brown meat well in non-stick pan or in heavy preheated pan. In a casserole arrange layers of meat, eggplant, and peppers, seasoning

each layer with onion, salt, pepper and oregano. Pour enough tomato juice and water over it to moisten it very well. Top with
tomato. Cover and bake in 350°F. oven for 1 hour. Remove cover
and bake 15 minutes more to brown top. Serves 3, including limited
vegetable (6 ounces cooked meat for women, 8 ounces for men).
Keeps for several days in refrigerator.

SUKIYAKI WITH SPINACH

   *2 pounds lean beef
   ½ pound sliced mushrooms
   *1 cup scallions with green tops, cut up
   3 celery stalks, cut up
   *2 medium onions (optional; dehydrated onion flakes
       may be substituted)
   1 cup canned bean sprouts, drained
   1 teaspoon sugar substitute
   ⅓ cup soy sauce
   1 chicken bouillon cube
   ½ cup hot water
   ½ pound spinach, washed, stems removed

Cut steaks into thin slices; brown meat well. Add mushrooms, scallions, celery, onion, bean sprouts and sugar substitute. Pour soy
sauce over mixture. Add bouillon cube dissolved in hot water. Heat
to boiling; then reduce heat. Simmer uncovered, stirring occasionally,
10 to 12 minutes or until vegetables are almost tender. Add spinach
leaves. Continue cooking 5 minutes longer, stirring occasionally or
until vegetables are crisply tender; do not overcook. Serves 4 at
dinner, including meat and 1 limited vegetable for each serving.

   * *Limited food—see Menu Plan, p. 18-20, for legal amount.*

PEPPER STEAK

   *2 pounds (or 4 portions) shoulder steak
    2 cups bouillon (or 3 cubes dissolved in 2 cups
     water)
    1 clove garlic
    2 tablespoons soy sauce
    1 teaspoon salt
    2 green peppers (cut up)

Slice steak into pieces ¼-inch thick and brown in large preheated iron pan over moderately high flame stirring constantly, about 2 minutes. Add 2 cups bouillon, garlic, soy sauce and salt. Cover and cook 5 minutes on moderate flame. Stir in peppers and cook additional 2 minutes.

CHINESE BEEF WITH SNOW PEAS

   *1 pound lean flank steak, sliced very thin across the
    grain
   *8 ounces frozen snow peas or Italian green beans
    ½ cup water
    Freshly grated black pepper
    Dash of sugar substitute
    ½ teaspoon MSG
    2 teaspoons soy sauce
    2 thin slices fresh ginger root or ½ teaspoon
     powdered ginger

Heat a heavy dry skillet and brown beef quickly turning once. Put snow peas or beans in center of pan and cook them quickly too. Stir in remaining ingredients, cover pan and cook for 2 minutes (not longer). Serve promptly. Serves 2. Can be easily doubled, tripled, etc. Note: Of course you can substitute young French-style green beans, and add another limited vegetable.

BEEF RAGOUT W.W.

 *1 medium onion, chopped
  1 clove garlic, mashed
 *3 servings beef, cut into 1-inch cubes (all visible
     fat removed)
  1 teaspoon paprika
  Salt and pepper to taste
 *2 tomatoes, chopped (optional; 1 cup tomato juice
     may be substituted)
  1 cup diced celery
  ½ ounce dried black mushrooms

Brown onion with garlic in preheated heavy dry skillet; keep turning so they do not burn. Discard garlic. Add beef and season with paprika, salt and pepper. Cook over medium flame, stirring to brown meat. Add tomatoes and celery. Cook 15 minutes. Meanwhile soak mushrooms in boiling hot water for 15 minutes. Add to ragout and cook 15 minutes longer. Three servings meat and limited vegetable. This reheats well; may be refrigerated two or three days.

HUNGARIAN GOULASH

 *2 portions boneless top round of beef, cut in
     1-inch cubes
  ½ cup beef broth
 *3 tablespoons Tomato Sauce (see index)
  2 stalks celery, sliced
  ½ diced green pepper
  1 clove garlic
 *2 medium carrots, cut in 1-inch pieces
  1 teaspoon salt
  Dash pepper
  1 tablespoon paprika
  1 sweet pimento
  1 bay leaf
  1 teaspoon caraway seeds

Put all ingredients except carrots into large iron pot. Cover and simmer 2½ hours. Add carrots and simmer another 30 minutes or until tender. If necessary add more beef broth. Two servings, each including meat and limited vegetable. Note: May be prepared without carrots, and another limited vegetable used instead.

BRAISED BEEF ROLL-UPS

   *Lean beef, cut in very thin slices: 2 servings
   Salt and pepper to taste
   1 green pepper, chopped
   4 stalks celery, chopped
   *1 onion, chopped
   1 teaspoon poultry seasoning
   ¼ cup BBQ Dressing (see index for recipe)

Weigh uncooked beef, allowing 8 ounces for women, 10 ounces for men. Arrange beef slices on wax paper, sprinkle lightly with salt and pepper. Combine green pepper, celery, onion and poultry seasoning; divide stuffing over meat slices, roll up, and fasten with wooden picks. Arrange roll-ups in shallow pan. Bake in moderate oven about 1½ hours. Baste with BBQ Dressing.

BOILED BEEF DINNER IN ONE POT

   *3 pounds lean first-cut brisket of beef
   Boiling water
   1 bay leaf
   ½ teaspoon thyme
   *2 carrots, scraped clean
   1 tablespoon dehydrated onion flakes
   2 stalks celery with leaves
   12 peppercorns, slightly mashed
   1 cabbage, cut into wedges
   *3 cups yellow turnips, sliced

Remove all visible fat from beef. Cover with boiling water in kettle. Bring water to boil, reduce heat; spoon out grease and scum. Add remaining ingredients. Simmer 3 hours or so until meat is tender. Slice meat and weigh it (6 ounces cooked for women; 8 ounces cooked for men). Divide vegetables into portions and serve. Serves 8. Mustard pickle goes well with this. Note: This is a good meal for family service but individual weighed portions can be packed in small containers, frozen, and reheated over low heat.

POT ROAST

  *Pot roast of beef in one piece totaling 4 servings
   1 teaspoon salt
   ⅛ teaspoon pepper
   ½ teaspoon ground ginger
   1 clove garlic, minced
  *1 carrot, cut up
   ¼ cup coarsely chopped parsley
   ½ cup water
  *½ cup tomato juice
  *1 onion, sliced
   2 stalks celery, sliced
  *½ cup peas
  *1 whole tomato, quartered

Cut visible fat from roast. Combine salt, pepper, and ginger and rub mixture thoroughly into meat. Heat a heavy Dutch oven and brown meat thoroughly on all sides over moderate flame. Add remaining ingredients (except whole tomato). Cover tightly and cook over very low heat about 3 hours until meat is tender. Remove meat and let it cool slightly to make slicing easier. Add tomato and continue to cook about 5 minutes until tomato is softened. This freezes well. Serves 4. Includes limited vegetable.

  * *Limited food—see Menu Plan, p. 18-20, for legal amount.*

ORIENTAL FRUIT CHOW

> *1 pound sirloin steak, 1 inch thick, cut in narrow
>   strips
> *1 medium onion, cut in wedges
> *1 5-ounce can bamboo shoots, drained
>   ½ cup bean sprouts, drained
>   1 3-ounce can broiled sliced mushrooms, drained
>   ½ teaspoon sugar substitute
>   ½ cup condensed beef broth
>   ¼ cup soy sauce
> *2 sliced peaches

Brown meat, half at a time, in hot skillet without fat. Turn pieces
so they don't burn. Add next 6 ingredients. Cover; simmer 5 minutes. Add soy sauce and cook and stir 10 minutes more. Add
peaches; cover and cook through. Makes 2 servings, and uses dinner allowance of beef and limited vegetable, plus fruit serving, for
each diner.

BROILED HAMBURGER

You can't beat a plain broiled *hamburger, made from half a pound
of lean round steak, sirloin or neck and tenderloin (leave the fat
in the pan), topped with hot sautéed mushrooms—unless you prefer
it with Creole Sauce or Sauce Chambord. And why not add a cold
sliced garden tomato (limited vegetable) on which you have sprinkled chopped dill or chives?

STORING HAMBURGER

Keep refrigerated for no more than two days, or store in freezer and
use within two to three months. Do not refreeze hamburger once it
has thawed. Do not press flat while cooking (you are squeezing out
juice).

CHOPPED SIRLOIN, CHINESE STYLE

> *2 pounds chopped sirloin
> Garlic salt or powder
> 1 green pepper
> 1 or 2 stalks celery
> ¼ cup toasted onion flakes, soaked in water
> ½ cup soy sauce
> 1 can bean sprouts

Shape four large or eight small hamburgers. Brown near flame of broiler. Transfer (without fat) to a large pan when lightly browned. Cut up and add all remaining ingredients. Cover and steam for 10 minutes. Serves 4 (weigh your portion).

MEAT LOAF

> *½ pound lean ground veal
> *½ pound lean ground beef
> ½ cup green peppers, minced fine
> ½ cup finely chopped or puréed green beans
> 3 tablespoons juice scraped from cut onion
> ½ teaspoon oregano
> ½ teaspoon paprika
> ½ teaspoon MSG
> Salt
> Pepper
> Water to moisten

Knead meat. Add finely minced green peppers, green beans, onion and other seasonings. Moisten lightly with water. Shape into loaf and bake, about 1 hour at 375° F. Baste with Blender Sauce, Louisiana style, or BBQ Baste. Serves 2.

* *Limited food—see Menu Plan, p. 18-20, for legal amount.*

SAUERBRATEN

1 cup vinegar
1 cup water
½ teaspoon salt
5 peppercorns
⅛ teaspoon cloves
3 bay leaves
*2 onions, chopped (if omitted add onion flakes
     for seasoning)
*2 carrots, sliced
*Beef chuck, brisket or top round in one piece
     totaling 4 allowed portions

Bring first 8 ingredients to a boil to make a marinade. Place meat in a bowl. Pour marinade over it. Refrigerate 2-3 days, turning the meat frequently. Drain meat, reserving marinade. Brown meat over low heat in very hot non-stick pan. Add marinade. Cover and cook over low heat for 2-3 hours. *Skim off fat* before serving (soak up with paper napkins or towels). Note: Onions and carrots may be omitted and other allowed vegetables substituted.

BEEF ROMANO

*2 pounds lean boneless round beef
½ cup bouillon
2 tablespoons wine vinegar
2 tablespoons water
1 tablespoon dehydrated onion flakes
1 clove garlic, chopped
¼ teaspoon oregano
¼ teaspoon celery seed
Salt
5 peppercorns, cracked
1 clove
1 bay leaf
*1 cup tomato juice

Be sure to remove visible fat from beef. Combine all remaining ingredients except tomato juice and marinate beef overnight. Next morning pour into baking dish, add tomato juice and bake, covered, for 2½ hours or until tender. Cool and skim off all fat. Slice, weigh, and serve. To serve hot, heat sauce and add beef slices but do not let them boil. This freezes well. Four servings.

BORSHT WITH MEAT

    *3 pounds lean beef (shoulder or round steak)
     1 large head cabbage, shredded
    *1 large onion
    *2½ cups canned whole tomatoes (no spices added),
        or fresh tomatoes
     ½ teaspoon salt
     Sour salt (or lemon juice)
     Sugar substitute to taste
     ½-1 teaspoon Gravy Master (for coloring)
     Water to cover cabbage

Combine and cook in large soup kettle for at least 3 hours on low flame (or in pressure cooker for about 45 minutes). Prepare the day before serving. Refrigerate and remove any solidified fat. Slice meat, weigh it and serve in hot borsht. Allow 6 ounces cooked beef for women; 8 ounces for men. Count onion as 1 serving and tomatoes as 5 servings of limited vegetables. Makes 6 dinner servings.

(Other recipes for Borsht are given on pages 186 and 187.)

Invited out? Before leaving for the big party, wedding reception, banquet, etc., eat your legal dinner. Then you can resist the smorgasbord and tremendous spread that follows. Just play with the food on your plate and stick to celery sticks, radishes, and a Bloody Mary or two (see recipe on p. 200). And learn how to dance—now you'll be able to!

HAMBURGER MEAL IN ONE DISH

> *1½ pounds lean hamburger meat (chopped round
>   steak is good)
> ½ cup finely chopped celery
> 1 cup Piquant Mushrooms (see index for recipe)
> *1½ cups tomato juice
> 1 cup water
> Freshly ground pepper
> 9 ounces frozen young green beans, cooked and
>   drained

Heat a large heavy iron skillet without adding fat, brown meat and celery stirring often. Transfer to casserole, draining off all fat. Add mushrooms, tomato juice, water, freshly ground pepper, and green beans. Bake at 350°F. for 30 minutes. Serves 3.

STUFFED PEPPERS

> *1 pound lean ground beef or half beef and half veal
> ¼ teaspoon salt
> ⅛ teaspoon pepper
> Onion powder to taste
> 1 clove garlic, pressed
> ½ pound mushrooms, cooked and chopped
> 1 teaspoon crushed leaf sage
> 1½ tablespoons chopped parsley
> 4 tablespoons water
> 6 green peppers, medium size
> 2 packages bouillon dissolved in 1 cup hot water

Preheat oven to 350°F. Mix chopped meat with salt, pepper, onion, garlic, mushrooms, leaf sage and parsley. Moisten slightly with water. Divide into 6 equal parts. Wash and remove tops of 6 medium-size, firm green peppers. Discard seeds and pith. Soften by

* *Limited food—see Menu Plan, p. 18-20, for legal amount.*

dropping them in boiling water for 5 minutes. Fill cavities with ground meat mixture. Place in a baking dish, pour in bouillon (or tomato juice if you have not used your maximum daily allowance of 12 ounces) and bake until peppers are tender, about 25 minutes. Peppers may be frozen in 6 individual servings, each counting as two ounces of cooked meat. Do not bake before freezing. Set on tray in freezer and pack in freezer bags when solidly frozen.

STUFFED CABBAGE (SWEET AND SOUR)

*1 pound lean ground beef
¼ teaspoon salt
⅛ teaspoon pepper
1 small green pepper, grated
Juice scraped from cut onion
1 clove garlic, pressed
1 tablespoon soy sauce
4 tablespoons ice water
1 medium-sized cabbage
*1½ cups tomato juice
*1 cup whole canned tomatoes
¾ cup water
¼ teaspoon salt
⅛ teaspoon pepper
¼ teaspoon onion powder
1 packet bouillon
¼ teaspoon sour salt, to taste
½ teaspoon sugar substitute, or to taste
1 cup canned sauerkraut
¾ cup water

Mix first 8 ingredients well. Set aside. Cut center core out of cabbage and place in bowl under very hot tap water until leaves are soft and separating. If water is not very hot plunge cabbage into boiling water for a few minutes for the same results. Separate cabbage leaves and wrap around meat balls (about 8 small balls). In bottom of cooking pot mix remaining ingredients. Gently place cabbage rolls into this liquid and boil about 1 hour covered or until cabbage is very tender. By dividing the cabbage into 4 servings at dinner, you will be able to include 2 broiled frankfurters or any other half portion of meat or fish, and half portion of vegetable.

Who says Veal has to be dull?

...not when you use the following W.W. recipes.

VEAL PILAFF

*Veal differs from best quality beeksteak in that veal needs pepping up with marinades and seasonings, ad libbed. Now as you know, ad lib means to improvise, extemporize and ignore the script. But here are some cues from the stage prompter—veal can be very effective when marinated overnight and cooked in a sauce made of *one grated turnip, *one grated carrot, a handful of celery leaves, 2 tablespoons lemon juice, onion powder or flakes, parsley and thyme, and a few tablespoons bouillon. (All limited vegetables must be counted, of course.)

COLD VEAL SALAD

> *Cooked veal (weigh legal portions)
> *Unpeeled red apples (1 for each serving)
> Dices of celery
> Coarsely chopped young green beans
> 1 tablespoon pickle liquid
> Dash salt

Combine all ingredients and refrigerate before serving. Serve in lettuce cups. (Weigh veal and count fruit in daily allowance.) Serve with Tomato French Dressing, Chambord Sauce, or any preferred sauce you have stocked in your refrigerator.

VEALBURGERS

Get the meat man who thinks you are an angel to grind up *veal and weigh it into 8-ounce units. Freeze with layers of foil or wax paper separating each unit. Broil like hamburgers. Serve with Creole Sauce, Chinese Sweet and Sour Sauce, or Sauce Chambord (see index for recipe).

VEAL ROAST

Order a boneless *veal roast. Sprinkle spices—onion powder, garlic, salt, pepper, paprika, mace if you have it—on large sheet of wax paper. Roll roast in this (clever trick—covers whole roast). Transfer roast to large roasting pan. Add 1 cup bouillon, cover with tin foil, insert meat thermometer, and bake until done in 325° F. oven. Weigh each serving.

Limited food—see Menu Plan, p. 18-20, for legal amount.

BROILED VEAL CHOPS

A good quick recipe popular with Weight Watchers calls for buying tender *veal chops, seasoning both sides with seasoning salt, and broiling until brown on both sides. Weigh before serving. Sometime you might try a sauce made of finely cut parsley and dill mixed with lemon juice and spread over the broiled chop. And another idea—marjoram and rosemary go well with veal.

BRAISED LOIN OF VEAL

     *3 pounds loin veal
     ¼ teaspoon pepper
     1 veal knuckle
     1½ teaspoons salt
     *2 onions, sliced, or onion powder
     *2 carrots, sliced
     2 stalks celery
     2 sprigs parsley
     1 bay leaf
     1 teaspoon thyme
     2 cups instant beef broth

Trim the veal and rub the salt and pepper into it. Place the onions, carrots, celery, parsley, bay leaf and thyme on the bottom of a Dutch oven. Place the veal knuckle on veal over it. Roast at 450° for 25 minutes. Stir in the broth. Roast 30 minutes basting frequently, then cover the pan. Reduce heat to 350° F. and roast 2 hours longer or until tender. Baste occasionally. Discard everything but the veal. Slice veal, weigh it and serve allowed portion.

BROILED VEAL CHOPS WITH MUSHROOMS

Choose young, white *veal chops with bone, allowing 10 ounces for women, 2 ounces more for men. Put under preheated broiler—10 minutes on each side for well-done veal. Place on hot platter, sprinkle with salt and pepper. Serve with fresh Mushroom Sauce. Good with a salad made of well-washed young spinach leaves tossed with Creole Sauce or Tomato French Dressing W.W.

VEAL AND PEPPERS

*2 servings veal
*1 onion, chopped
 1 green pepper, cut up
 Paprika
 1 clove mashed garlic
*1 tomato, cut up
 Chopped dill

Brown veal in hot heavy skillet (use no fat). Push to side and brown onion and green pepper with paprika and garlic in center of same pan. Add tomato (to make 1 limited vegetable with onion) and sauté gently for a few minutes. Cover and simmer gently until done. Season with chopped dill before serving at dinner. Two servings, including limited vegetable.

VEAL FRICASSEE

*1 pound boneless lean veal
*½ cup sliced carrots
 1 cup celery
 2 tablespoons dehydrated onion flakes
 2 tablespoons chopped parsley
 1 bay leaf
 Water or stock to cover
*½ cup peas
*Buttermilk

Season veal, cut into pieces and brown in heavy dry preheated skillet. Add carrots, celery, onion, parsley, bay leaf and water or stock. Cover tightly and cook in 350° F. oven 45 to 60 minutes or until meat is tender. Transfer to serving platter. Reduce liquid by boiling it down, then add peas and cook gently. Just before serving, pour a little buttermilk into sauce. Pour over veal and bring quickly to the table for two hungry diners. Includes limited vegetables.

VEAL BIRDS

Wrap thin slices of *veal—check weight and do not exceed allowed portion—around cooked asparagus sprinkled with minced parsley, or stuff with Mushroom Purée (both unlimited vegetables). Tie or secure with toothpicks, season to taste, and brown in preheated heavy skillet. Add a little *tomato juice, cover and simmer on top of stove or bake in 350° F. oven for 1 hour. Add liquid (water, consommé or more *tomato juice) in small amounts to keep veal from drying.

Note: Cooked carrots may be used in this recipe, but it is a limited vegetable.

VEAL SCALLOPINE

1 cup bouillon
*1 pound veal, cut up
1 clove garlic, finely minced
1 4-ounce can sliced mushrooms
*1 tablespoon thick tomato sauce (made from 4
   tablespoons tomato juice boiled down almost
   to a paste)
1 small bay leaf
⅛ teaspoon oregano

Heat ¼ cup bouillon and add veal. Brown quickly on both sides. Then add remaining bouillon, garlic, undrained mushrooms, tomato sauce, bay leaf and oregano. Cover tightly and cook over low heat 10 minutes. Season to taste with salt and pepper and serve.

VEAL A LA KING

½ green pepper, diced
¼ pound mushrooms
*½ cup skim milk
½ cup stock
¼ cup diced pimento
Salt
Pepper
12 ounces cut-up cooked veal

Cook pepper and mushrooms in a hot dry skillet for about 5 minutes, turning constantly. Add milk, stock, pimento and seasonings, and cool gently, stirring constantly. Just before serving, add veal and heat it up but do not let it boil. (Boiling a cooked meat always seems to extract its juices and make it tough.) Serves 2 women at dinner. Add 2 ounces veal for each man's serving.

VEAL RAGOUT

For each diner, cook half *onion, sliced, in 3 tablespoons bouillon. Add ¼ cup mushrooms, ¼ cup *tomato juice, 1 green pepper (cut in rings), marjoram, garlic, salt and pepper to taste and continue cooking for 10 minutes. Meanwhile brown under broiler thinly-sliced *veal (allowed portion) and cut into small pieces before putting into sauce. Simmer until veal is well done; stir in ¼ cup uncooked *peas, cook only until done, and serve. This ragout includes limited vegetable.

VEAL STEW FOR ONE

*8 ounces lean veal cubes for stewing
1 package instant beef or vegetable broth
   dissolved in 6 ounces water
*8 ounces tomato juice
¼ cup dehydrated onion flakes
¼ pound mushrooms
Approximately 3 large stalks of celery, cut up
1 tablespoon chopped parsley
Another unlimited vegetable: French-style green
   beans, asparagus, etc.
Salt
Pepper
Garlic powder
1 bay leaf

Place meat in saucepan. Add broth, tomato juice, onion and seasonings. Bring slowly to a boil. Simmer, covered, for about 1 hour. Then add remaining ingredients; cook until vegetables are tender, ½ hour. To have for two meals, double recipe. Tastes even better the second day.

BAKED FILET OF VEAL WITH VEGETABLES

Weigh *veal roast, allowing ½ pound raw for each woman; 10 ounces for each man. Cut off as much fat as possible from veal roast. Season meat with garlic, salt, oregano, parsley flakes, etc. Line baking pan with aluminum foil to make it easier to clean afterwards. Put meat in pan and surround with onion flakes and *stewing tomatoes (one for each portion), green pepper, mushrooms (all vegetables fresh, not canned). Then pour *tomato juice over all. Let roast for at least two hours or according to size of meat. If you have used day's allowance of tomato juice, cover roast with beef stock or water.

CONTINENTAL VEAL

        3 teaspoons soy sauce
     *2 pounds lean veal, cubed, washed and patted dry
     *2 onions, diced
      1 clove garlic, diced fine
      1 cup water, stock or *tomato juice
      ¼ teaspoon sugar substitute
      ½ teaspoon salt to taste
      ½ teaspoon pepper to taste
      1 teaspoon rosemary or marjoram
     *2 small carrots, sliced thin
      4 large peppers
      2 small cans mushroom or ½ pound
        fresh mushrooms
      1 teaspoon grated lemon rind
      Water

Measure soy sauce into large non-stick skillet and brown veal, onions, and garlic on medium flame, stirring often to prevent sticking, about 15 minutes. Add water or stock or tomato juice and 4 seasonings, cover and cook until veal is tender (slow fire) about 1 hour. Fifteen minutes before done add carrots, green pepper and mushrooms. Just before serving, stir in lemon rind. Add water (or stock or tomato juice) as necessary during cooking. Serves 4, including limited vegetable.

Note: May be frozen in individual freezer container and reheated as necessary.

DINNER A DEUX

Bloody Mary, p. 200
Continental Veal (half recipe)
Apples and Sauerkraut (half recipe), p. 243
Dilled Cucumber Slices, p. 161
Maple Bavarian Cream, p. 274

VEAL EN PAPILLOTE

Buy young *veal chops (10 ounces for women, 12 ounces for men). Brown in a hot dry skillet until golden brown on both sides. Combine powdered thyme, nutmeg and finely chopped parsley with salt and pepper and a few drops of cayenne pepper. Sprinkle chops with these seasonings. Cut a large heart-shaped piece of aluminum foil to fit each chop, leaving a margin of several inches all around. Put a layer of Mushroom Purée or Piquant Mushrooms (see index for recipes) on the paper, add seasoned chop, top with a layer of Creole Sauce. Fold so that steam and juices do not escape. Put into a shallow pan and bake 30 minutes at 325° F. Serve at once.

Cook Veal chops in hot, dry, skillet until golden brown on both sides

* *Limited food—see Menu Plan, p. 18-20, for legal amount.*

Creole sauce

Cut heart-shaped piece of aluminum foil for each chop.

Sprinkle browned chops with seasoning mixture

Mushroom Purée

Fold aluminum foil to prevent steam and juices escaping.

VEAL CHOW MEIN

*1 pound veal
2 tablespoons soy sauce
½ teaspoon salt
1 cup beef bouillon
3 tablespoons dehydrated onion flakes
2 cups thinly sliced celery
1 pound canned bean sprouts, drained, and washed
  in cold water
½ teaspoon ground ginger

Cook veal with soy sauce, salt and bouillon, in covered pan, until meat is tender. Add onions, celery, bean sprouts and ginger. Cook 10 minutes. Serves to 2.

VEAL-STUFFED MUSHROOMS

Buy medium or large-size mushrooms. Remove stems and reserve them for another use. Stuff caps with cooked, chopped, seasoned *veal. Pour a thin layer of *tomato juice on a cookie sheet. Place stuffed mushrooms on this. Sprinkle a bit of tomato juice and chopped parsley over mushrooms. Bake at 375° F. for 15 minutes. (Note: weigh the veal before using; women are allowed 6 ounces, cooked, at dinner; men, 8 ounces.)

VEAL AND CHICKEN ROULADE

      *Chicken breasts, boned; 2 allowed portions
      ½ teaspoon garlic salt
      Dash of pepper
      ½ teaspoon oregano
      ½ teaspoon leaf thyme
      ½ cup chicken broth
      1 tablespoon grated onion
      1 bay leaf
      *Veal; 1 serving, cut in 2 pieces

Remove skin from breasts. Cut lengthwise into 4 strips about 1 inch wide. Combine garlic salt, pepper, oregano, and thyme; coat chicken with mixture. Brown under broiler. Put in skillet with chicken broth, onion, and bay leaf. Cover; simmer 20 minutes or until tender. Remove bay leaf. Remove and wrap each piece of chicken in veal; fasten with wooden pick. Put chicken-veal rolls back in skillet, simmer 5 minutes. Serve at once with sauce on each. Makes 3 servings.

VEAL CHAMBORD

Heat Chambord Sauce (see index) with cut-up slivers of pimento. Combine allowed weight of cooked, cut-up *veal with heated sauce and serve at once.

VEAL WITH CHICKEN LIVERS
(Scallopine al Fegato)

    *¼ pound thin veal, pounded thin
    *¼ pound chicken livers, diced
    *1 chopped tomato (or use Tomato Sauce W.W. and
        another limited vegetable)
    ¼ teaspoon thyme
    1 teaspoon salt
    ½ teaspoon freshly ground pepper

Heat a heavy iron skillet and brown veal and livers over moderately high heat, turning often. Add tomatoes, thyme, and salt and pepper. Cook over medium heat 10 minutes longer until veal is tender. Serves 1.

Note: Veal slices, browned first, may be stuffed with remaining ingredients which have been cooked together. After stuffing, they may be simmered in water or chicken stock.

VEAL SURPRISE

    *1 pound veal cutlet, cut into thin strips, 3 x 5 inches
    Salt and pepper
    *½ carrot, cut into strips
    *½ onion, sliced
    ½ cup beef bouillon
    *1 cup tomato juice

Season veal slices with salt and pepper. On each slice place a small strip of carrot and 2 pieces of onion. Wrap veal around vegetables and secure with toothpicks. Brown veal rolls in beef bouillon. Add tomato juice. Cover and cook slowly for 1 hour. Two servings, including limited vegetable.

    * *Limited food—see Menu Plan, p. 18-20, for legal amount.*

WHITE DRAGON VEAL

> *1 pound tenderloin veal
> 1 tablespoon soy sauce
> 5 dried Japanese mushrooms
> ⅓ cup green pepper, diced
> *⅔ cup sliced bamboo shoots
> 3 tablespoons dehydrated onion flakes
> 2 tablespoons chicken stock
> 3 slices ginger, crushed and minced
> 1 clove garlic, crushed and minced
> Salt and pepper to taste

Cut the veal into pieces 2½ x 2 x 1-inch. Brush them with soy sauce. Let marinate for 15 minutes. At the same time, cover the mushrooms with water and let them soak for 15 minutes. Heat a non-stick frying pan, add veal and stir-fry quickly. Remove it while it is still rare. Drain mushrooms (save liquid), cut them in half, and stir-fry in same pan with the green pepper. After a minute or two, add bamboo shoots, liquid in which mushrooms soaked, onion, ginger, garlic, salt and pepper. Stir-fry for two minutes more. Make a well in center of pan and return veal to it to cook until veal is tender, but still moist and juicy. Two servings at dinner, including meat and limited vegetable.

ROAST VEAL HASH

Grind leftover cooked *veal (weigh it first so you do not exceed meat allowance). Mix with chopped onion flakes, horseradish, Worcestershire sauce, salt, pepper and MSG and *some skim milk or *tomato juice to bind. Pack lightly in casserole. Bake at 350° F. for about ¾ hour, or heat under broiler. Serve with Hot Sauce.

HOT SAUCE

Sauté minced garlic, and chopped green pepper in hot dry skillet. Add ½ cup each chopped celery, and drained canned pieces of mushrooms, *tomato juice, a few drops Tabasco sauce, Worcestershire sauce and any desired seasonings; simmer 10 minutes. Serve hot.

VEAL AND KIDNEY SHISH-KEBAB

  *1 pound veal kidneys
  *1 pound veal for stewing
   Meat tenderizer
   2 large green peppers
  *4 medium onions
   ½ teaspoon salt
   ½ teaspoon pepper
   ½ teaspoon garlic powder
   ½ teaspoon onion powder
   ¾ cup soy sauce

Wash and clean kidneys thoroughly by removing membrane from outside (usually these have been removed when you buy them). Cut in half lengthwise. Cut as much fat out of inside of kidney as you can. Soak cleaned kidney in salted water holding 2 tablespoons vinegar for 30 minutes. While kidneys are soaking sprinkle meat tenderizer on veal cubes following directions on bottle. Cut green peppers into 2-inch cubes. Peel and cut onions into quarters. Remove kidneys from water and rinse with cold water. Place all ingredients in bowl and cover with remaining spices and soy sauce. Marinate overnight. Alternate meat and vegetables on skewers. Broil until brown and tender turning and basting with remaining marinade. Four dinner servings, including limited vegetable.

A "blitz" reducing diet is useless. In most cases, you will backslide and revert to old eating habits. Stay on the Weight Watchers program and follow your Menu Plan, pages 18-20.

KIDNEYS

 *1 pound veal kidneys
 Cold salted water with 2 tablespoons vinegar
 Green pepper
 *Tomato juice
 ½ teaspoon chopped dill
 Salt
 Pepper, freshly ground

Cut 1 pound veal kidneys into 1-inch slices and cut away with scissors all white tissue. Soak slices in cold water holding 2 tablespoons vinegar for 30 minutes. Drain and arrange on skewers, alternating with cubes of green pepper. Lay skewered kidneys in shallow dish and cover with tomato juice seasoned with dill, salt and pepper. Let stand an hour or longer, turning occasionally. Remove from sauce and broil slowly until browned. Turn them to brown all sides. Baste with marinade several times as they broil. Serve hot. Two servings at dinner.

KIDNEY STEW

 *1 pound kidneys (lamb, veal or beef)
 Water to cover with 2 teaspoons vinegar
 1 diced pimento
 1 diced green pepper
 1 minced garlic clove
 1 chopped stalk of celery (including leaves)
 *1 cup tomato juice
 1 teaspoon salt
 ¼ teaspoon freshly ground pepper
 Drop or two Tabasco sauce

Cut kidneys into lengthwise pieces, cut away all white tissue with scissors, and soak in water for 30 minutes with 2 teaspoons vinegar. Drain and rinse. Cut into ¾-inch slices. Combine remaining ingredients, bring to boil, add kidneys and cook 30 minutes. Two dinner servings.

HEART CHOP SUEY

Veal, beef or lamb hearts are full of nutrition. It is surprising how little this meat is appreciated.

    *1½ pound heart
    2 whole cloves
    1 garlic clove
    ¼ cup chopped celery
    10 peppercorns
    1 large bay leaf
    ¼ teaspoon powdered thyme
    2 tablespoons lemon juice
    1 cup sliced mushrooms
    Salt and pepper to taste

Wash the heart in plenty of water and remove any fat, veins and membranes. Cover with boiling water and add cloves, garlic, celery, peppercorns, bay leaf and thyme. Bring to boil and remove scum with a spoon. Cook for 3 hours until meat is tender and very little stock is left. Add lemon juice and mushrooms, and continue cooking another half hour. Season with salt and pepper. Three dinner servings.

CALVES LIVER ALLA VENEZIANA FOR ONE

    *1 medium onion, sliced
    ½ cup chicken broth
    *8 ounces calves liver
    ½ sliced green pepper
    ½ teaspoon salt
    ½ teaspoon dehydrated red and green pepper flakes
    ¼ teaspoon crushed red pepper
    2 tablespoons chopped parsley

   * *Limited food—see Menu Plan, p. 18-20, for legal amount.*

Simmer onion in chicken broth until liquid is evaporated. Using a pair of scissors cut liver into julienne strips, about ¾ inches wide. Add liver to onions with sliced peppers and seasoning (except parsley). Cook over moderately high heat, tossing occasionally until liver is cooked on all sides but still pink inside (about 4 to 5 minutes). Stir in parsley and serve. (Helen Quat, author of *The Wonderful World of Freezer Cooking,* and a successful Weight Watcher contributed this recipe. It can be easily multiplied to serve the average family.)

CHOPPED CHICKEN LIVER

> *1 onion, sliced
> *1 pound chicken livers, washed and halved
> Salt
> Freshly ground pepper
> Pinch cayenne pepper or Tabasco sauce
> Pinch curry powder (optional)
> Dash nutmeg (optional)
> Lettuce
> Radishes

In a heavy, hot, dry skillet make a layer of onion slices. Spread livers over onion. Cover and cook until liver is done but not dried out. (Cut one—it should be evenly tan, inside and out.) There should be a layer of liquid in the bottom of the pan. If there is more, remove livers and boil down remaining stock, until you have about ¼ cup. Cool livers, onions and stock. Season with salt, pepper and a pinch of cayenne pepper or Tabasco. A pinch of curry powder or a dash of nutmeg are optional seasonings. Put through fine blade of food grinder or purée in an electric blender with a little of the stock in which livers cooked to start it off. Serve on a lettuce leaf garnished with a slice of radish. Serves two at dinner; including one-half serving of a limited vegetable for each.

LIVER APPETIZER

Divide chopped chicken liver into 8 servings. Serve chicken liver in a ball set on lettuce leaves surrounded by assorted unlimited greens. Insert a slice of cucumber on top of ball. Count as 2 ounces of dinner meat. For men's dinner, add 8 ounces uncooked meat, or 6 ounces cooked meat. For women's or teenagers' dinner, add 6 ounces uncooked meat or 4 ounces cooked meat.

Chicken liver may also be set under broiler about 1 inch from heat and broiled for 7-10 minutes. A cooked pineapple slice makes a good bed for the liver.

Note: Chopped chicken liver may be frozen on sheet and stored in freezer container, with weight marked. However, the texture of the liver changes, so purée it in blender or chop fine when partially defrosted and just before serving.

CHICKEN-LIVER KEBABS

   *1 pound chicken livers
   *8 cherry tomatoes
    1½-inch squares of green pepper
    2 tablespoons Worcestershire sauce

Cut chicken livers in half; snip out any veiny parts or skin with scissors. Thread long thin skewers this way: Chicken liver half, cherry tomato, chicken liver half, pepper square, chicken liver half. Allow about ¼ inch between each. Place on rack in broiler pan; brush with part of the Worcestershire sauce. Broil, 6 inches from heat, 7 minutes; turn. Brush with remaining Worcestershire sauce, then continue broiling 7 minutes, or until done as you like it. Two dinner servings: meat and limited vegetable.

   * *Limited food—see Menu Plan, p. 18-20, for legal amount.*

LIVER AND MUSHROOMS FOR ONE

*8 ounces beef livers, cut in 2-inch pieces
4 fresh mushrooms
Salt and pepper
*1 tomato
2 tablespoons Tomato French Dressing W.W.

String a whole mushroom on a skewer, then a liver piece, then another mushroom, end with liver. Repeat. Sprinkle with salt and pepper and broil over charcoal (or under broiler). Turn as needed and serve on a bed of baked or broiled tomato slices—one whole tomato sliced, broiled and basted with Tomato French Dressing W.W. Dinner for one, includes limited vegetable.

CALVES LIVER KEBAB

*8 ounces calves liver
2 stalks celery, diced

Wipe calves liver with damp paper towel. String on skewers with celery dice. Broil quickly close to flame until liver is brown, turning as necessary. 1 serving.

LUNG AND ONION STEW A LA GRACE

*1 pound beef lung
*2 onions
1 teaspoon salt
½ teaspoon pepper
3 cups water

Wash lung and cut into cubes (about 3-inch size). Slice onion, add salt, pepper and water. Cook on high flame in heavy tightly-covered kettle about 2 hours or until lung is tender and most of water has disappeared. Add additional water during cooking if necessary. When ready to be eaten lung should be tender and there should be only about ½ cup thick liquid or gravy on bottom of pan. Two servings, including limited vegetable.

BRAISED LAMB POT ROAST

    Salt, pepper, rosemary
*1 boned lean lamb roast, 3 pounds
*2 carrots
*1 cup peas
*2 large onions or 10 small white onions
*1 cup tomato sauce (2 cups tomato juice boiled
    down)
    Mashed clove of garlic

Rub seasonings into roast. Brown in hot oven on roasting pan rack. Lift roast to center of large square of aluminum foil, surround with carrots cut in 1-inch slices, peas, and cut onions. Pull up sides of foil. Combine tomato sauce and garlic. Pour over meat and vegetables. Close foil and twist. Return to 325° F. oven and cook 1½ to 2 hours. For a barbecue supper: Place meat packet on outdoor grill to keep hot, or if desired, lift meat from foil packet to recrisp over coals, about 10 minutes. Weigh meat; serves six at dinner, including limited vegetable serving.

BROILED LAMB CHOPS OR MEDALLIONS

Remove visible fat, gristle, etc., from *lamb chops and add 2 ounces to the allowed portion (for bone). Or even better, ask the most agreeable butcher in the shop to cut medallions from the rack or loin of lamb, boned and trimmed, then weigh each one to give allowed amount for dinner (8 ounces uncooked for women, 10 ounces for men). Broil, topping first with a slice of apple, grapefruit, or orange (cut from one serving of your allowed fruit) and you will have a dish to be proud of.

Lamb chops with fat and gristle removed

make cut ½ way through to make pocket

Place mint leaves in pocket. Top chops with apple, orange or grapefruit slices. Broil.

Delicious... pretty too!

OTHER IDEAS

Put fresh mint leaves between thin *lamb chops before broiling, or have a pocket cut in thicker ones to hold the mint. Broil.

LAMBURGERS

Have all the fat removed from an inexpensive cut of *lamb (breast, shoulder, shanks). Put through meat chopper, weigh, add seasonings, shape into patty and broil like hamburgers.

LAMB CHAMBORD

Cut up lean roast *lamb (weigh it first) and add to heated Chambord Sauce (see index).

LAMB-STUFFED ZUCCHINI

   6 small zucchini
*2 cups minced cooked lamb
   2 tablespoons grated onion
   1 tablespoon minced parsley
   Oregano
   Enough sauce (Cooked Barbecue Sauce, Creole or
      Mushroom Sauce—see index for recipe)
      to moisten
   ¾ cup water

Remove pulp from zucchini with an apple corer. Combine lamb, onion, minced parsley, oregano and sauce. Season to taste with salt and use to stuff zucchini. Put zucchini into shallow baking dish and pour in water (or tomato juice if you have any left from day's allowance), seasoned with oregano. Bake at 350° F. for ½ hour or until zucchini are tender. Serves 3 dinners.

   Note: You can also cut zucchini in half and scoop out some of inside. Leftover filling can be baked in the same baking dish.

LAMB SKEWERS

Any of the veal kebabs can be used with *lamb (see index for recipes). *Eggplant cubes and *cherry tomatoes are an excellent combination with chunks of lamb on a spit. Both eggplant and cherry tomatoes are limited vegetables.

ROAST LEG OF LAMB

*Lamb is a tender meat which roasts well. You may rub the leg of lamb with cut garlic or lemon, and insert slivers of garlic or herbs under the skin using a pointed knife. Roast 30-35 minutes to the pound in slow oven (300°F.). Weigh portion after carving. Good with Mint Sauce, p. 229.

BARBECUED FRANKFURTERS-SAUERKRAUT

¼ cup dehydrated onion flakes
½ cup chopped green pepper
¼ cup chicken stock
*2 pounds frankfurters, boiled first to drain fat,
    then gashed in places
*¾ cup tomato sauce (1½ cups tomato juice
    cooked down)
½ teaspoon Worcestershire sauce
1 teaspoon prepared mustard
½ teaspoon salt
1 can (1 pound, 11 ounces) sauerkraut, drained

Cook onion and green pepper until tender in saucepan with chicken stock. Add frankfurters and brown lightly. Combine tomato sauce, Worcestershire sauce, mustard and salt. Add to frankfurters. Cook slowly about 10 minutes. Spoon sauerkraut into two-quart casserole. Arrange franks on sauerkraut and pour sauce over all. Cover tightly and bake in a 350° F. oven 20 minutes. Four dinner servings, or serve 8 servings and supplement with meat appetizer, or cut recipe in half to serve 2 or quarter to serve 1.

FRANKS PIQUANT

1 pound sauerkraut
*½ cup tomato juice
Onion flakes
1 teaspoon horseradish
*1 pound frankfurters, boiled or broiled
    first to drain off fat
1 pimento, cut into strips

Combine sauerkraut with tomato juice, onion and horseradish. Cook over moderate heat for 1 hour, then put into oven dish. Top with franks and pimento and place in 450° F. oven for 25 minutes. 2 dinner servings.

FRANKFURTER CASSEROLE CREOLE STYLE

    *1½ pounds frankfurters
    *1 onion, thinly sliced
     1 cup mushrooms, thinly sliced
     Salt
     Pepper
     Thyme
     Mace
     Nutmeg
     Garlic salt
     1 bay leaf
    *1 cup canned tomatoes
     1 large green pepper, seeded and sliced

Boil or broil frankfurters so fat drains off. Slice. Lay frankfurters in
a large casserole. Top with onion and mushrooms. Sprinkle salt
and pepper over mushrooms. Combine thyme, mace, nutmeg, garlic
salt and bay leaf and sprinkle over mushrooms. Pour tomatoes over
this. Arrange green pepper slices on tomatoes. Cover and bake at
350° F. for 50 minutes. Dinner for three, including limited vegetable.

FRANKS AND GREEN BEANS

    *1 pound frankfurters, cut in 2-inch pieces
     1 cup sliced celery
     Grated onion for seasoning
     ½ cup chicken broth
    *1½ cups tomato juice
     ¼ cup water
     ½ teaspoon granulated sugar substitute
     1 tablespoon vinegar
     2 teaspoons prepared mustard
     9 ounces frozen French-style green beans

Preheat a large heavy iron skillet without fat. Add pieces of frankfurters, and brown them on all sides. Pour off fat. Set frankfurters

aside. Cook celery and onion in chicken broth in same skillet until liquid is evaporated. Add remaining ingredients. Cover and simmer 30 minutes, stirring occasionally. A good Sunday dinner for two. When guests are present, multiply the recipe as needed.

FRANKS AND CABBAGE

    1 small cabbage
  *1 pound frankfurters
  *2 cups Tomato Sauce (see index for recipe)
    1 tablespoon dehydrated onion flakes
    2 tablespoons prepared mustard
    1 teaspoon Tabasco sauce
    1 teaspoon Worcestershire sauce
    ⅛ teaspoon black pepper

Boil cabbage until leaves are pliable. Remove outside leaves as they become soft (2 minutes). Let inside ones cook for 10 minutes. Wrap 1 large leaf around each frankfurter. Chop remaining cabbage fine. Arrange bundles in square casserole. Fill empty spots with cabbage. Bring to boil the remaining ingredients. Pour over bundles. Bake 45 minutes at 350° F. Dinner for two.

FRANKFURTER SANDWICH

Wrap a cooked *frankfurter in one leaf of Belgian endive cooked in water to soften. Spread with pickle relish.

Another good "sandwich"—wrap the cooked frankfurter in a pimento, spread with mustard, and enjoy.

FRANKS, APPLE AND CABBAGE

Combine 2 cups canned sauerkraut, 1 tart *apple cut fine, 1 teaspoon sugar substitute, and 1 pound *frankfurters. Cook 15-20 minutes or bake at 375° F. Dinner for two, including half portion of fruit.

SWEET AND SOUR FRANKFURTERS

> 2 teaspoons prepared mustard
> 1 teaspoon Tabasco or hot pepper sauce
> 1 teaspoon Worcestershire sauce
> 1 teaspoon sugar substitute
> 2 tablespoons white vinegar
> *2 tablespoons Tomato Sauce (see index for recipe)
> 1 tablespoon pickle relish
> ½ teaspoon paprika
> *1 pound franks, cooked or broiled first so fat
>   drains off

Cook together rapidly first 8 ingredients for 10 minutes. Pour over franks in casserole. Cover and bake 30-40 minutes at 375° F. Serves two.

BROILED OR BARBECUED CHICKEN

Broil or barbecue *chicken breasts, basting occasionally with chicken stock. When almost ready, brush with a mixture of soy sauce, lemon juice, 2 drops liquid sugar substitute, oregano, ⅛ teaspoon dry mustard and continue until tender, or barbecue outdoors.

CHICKEN CACCIATORA

> *2 pounds boneless chicken breasts, cut into 8 pieces
> 2 small green peppers
> 1 clove garlic
> 2 tablespoons finely chopped pimento
> 1 bay leaf
> Salt
> Pepper
> ¼ teaspoon dried thyme
> 6 sprigs parsley
> 1 to 1½ cups sliced mushrooms
> *2 cups stewed tomatoes

Combine all ingredients in saucepan. Simmer 30 minutes. Uncover and continue cooking until sauce is reduced to desired consistency. Dinner for 4; includes limited vegetable.

CORNISH HENS

Split *Cornish hens in half. Put *onion in bottom of pan. Place hens skin side up. Sprinkle with garlic, pepper, celery salt and paprika. Cover tightly with silver foil. Bake 1 hour. Take off cover. Baste and bake 15 mintues longer.

FRIED CHICKEN AND ONIONS

> *1 broiler-fryer (2½-3 pounds), cut in serving-size
>   pieces
> 1 teaspoon salt
> ⅛ teaspoon pepper
> *2 onions, peeled and sliced
> ½ cup water

Place chicken, skin side down, in a single layer in a large frying pan. Sprinkle with salt and pepper; place onion slices on top; cover tightly. (No need to add any fat.) Cook over low heat 30 minutes. Tilt lid slightly so liquid will evaporate; continue cooking 20 minutes longer, or until chicken is tender and golden. Place chicken on a heated serving platter, pushing onions back into pan. Stir in water, mixing with browned bits from bottom of pan (mushrooms may be added at this point and cooked until done). Cook until liquid evaporates. Spoon over chicken. Serve with green beans which are unlimited. Count onion. Three to four servings; use only white meat as Weight Watchers portion.

* *Limited food—see Menu Plan, p. 18-20, for legal amount.*

COLD HONG KONG CHICKEN

Roast or steam *chicken breasts. Weigh portion. Let cool without refrigerating it (flavor is better that way). Just before serving, put a thin coat of *buttermilk on bottom of individual platter. Cover with shredded Chinese cabbage or lettuce. Slice the chicken and arrange in weighed portions on Chinese cabbage. Cover with Chambord Sauce and serve.

MUSHROOMS STUFFED WITH MEAT

Prepare 8 large mushrooms, chop stems and cook them with ¼ cup sliced celery in water or chicken stock. Add 1 tablespoon curry powder, *2 ounces diced cooked white meat of chicken or veal and salt and pepper to taste. Fill caps with mixture. Top with *crumbs made from ½ slice luncheon bread. Bake until heated through and brown on top, and serve.

HOT CHICKEN OR TURKEY SALAD

        *1½ pounds diced cooked chicken or turkey,
            white meat
        1 cup consommé, mushroom liquid or water
        *1 cup boiled tiny white onions
        1 cup green beans, French style
        1 small can mushrooms
        1½ cups thinly sliced celery
        1 pimento, diced
        Salt and pepper
        *2 tomatoes, sliced

Heat consommé or liquid, add remaining ingredients (except tomatoes) and heat but do not boil (use low flame). Toss with fork to blend all ingredients, then turn into baking shells or cleaned half grapefruit shells. Bake in hot oven (400°F.) about 15 minutes. Serve with tomatoes. Four dinner servings for women; add 2 ounces for each man. Includes limited vegetable.

SPANISH CHICKEN

    *1 young chicken (3 pounds) cut into pieces
    *1½ cups tomatoes, chopped
    1 green pepper, chopped
    *1 onion, chopped
    ½ cup capers
    1 pimento, chopped
    Salt

Place all ingredients in pot with just enough water to cover. Cover and simmer 1½ hours. If there is too much liquid remove cover and cook until most of it is evaporated. Serves 4. Weight Watchers must use only white meat, weighed. This recipe includes limited vegetable.

WEIGHT WATCHERS' PAELLA

    *2 pounds breast of chicken, cut in serving-size
        pieces
    *1 large onion, chopped (1 cup)
    1 clove garlic, minced
    *6 small slices frankfurter (about 2 ounces) **diced and**
        browned to drain off fat
    2 teaspoons salt
    Dash sugar substitute
    ¼ teaspoon pepper
    ⅛ teaspoon crushed saffron
    *1 can (about 1 pound) tomatoes
    1½ cups water
    1 envelope instant chicken broth
        or 1 chicken bouillon cube
    *1 pound fresh shrimp, shelled and deveined
        (becomes 8 oz. cooked) *or* 1 package frozen
        deveined shelled raw shrimp
    1 can (4 ounces) pimentos, drained and cut in
        large pieces

Broil chicken: Broil chicken 4 inches from heat until golden brown, turning once. This should take about 10 minutes on each side. (Do not use fat which drains off.)

Make sauce: In a large kettle combine franks, onion, garlic, salt, sugar substitute, pepper, saffron, tomatoes, water and instant chicken broth mix. Bring to boil.

Prepare casserole: Arrange shrimps in 3-quart casserole, top with boiling sauce, add broiled chicken pieces and pimento and cook at 350°F. for 1 hour or until chicken is tender. Garnish with parsley and chopped scallions. 4 dinner servings which include limited vegetable.

Note: If you are wondering whether to count this as fowl or fish—it is fowl beyond a doubt.

CHICKEN WITH EGGPLANT

Follow recipe for Spanish Chicken but omit capers and pimento and add 1 diced, unpeeled *eggplant and generous seasoning of dried oregano.

STEAMED CHICKEN

Did you ever try steamed *chicken? Put a small chicken in a colander and set the colander in a large kettle holding boiling water (just enough so that chicken is not in water). Cover and let cook until chicken is soft. The tricky thing is to keep adding boiling water to the kettle so the steam continues to rise, because it's the steam that does the cooking. Then slice off the white meat (removing skin and bones) and serve over cooked and seasoned broccoli or chopped spinach topped with Sauce Chambord (see index). You're on your honor to consume just your "legal" portion of this tender, juicy poultry.

* *Limited food—see Menu Plan, p. 18-20, for legal amount.*

TURKEY MADRILENE LUNCHEON MOLD

    1 envelope unflavored gelatin
    1 cup water
 *12 ounces tomato juice
    2 tablespoons vinegar
    2 cucumbers
 *½ cup Sour Cream W.W.
 *12 ounces finely chopped cooked turkey,
       white meat
 *1 ounce diced Swiss cheese
    Pickle relish

Sprinkle gelatin over water in saucepan; place over low heat; stir until dissolved. Remove from heat; stir in tomato juice and vinegar. Measure 2 cups of gelatin mixture into medium-sized bowl; chill until syrupy. Cover bottom of 1½-quart mold with half the remaining gelatin mixture; chill until almost set. Cut cucumbers into fancy shapes with sharp knife or small hors d'oeuvre cutters. Arrange in design on almost-set gelatin. Carefully cover with second half of gelatin mixture. Chill until just set. Fold Sour Cream W.W., turkey, Swiss cheese, and pickle relish into syrupy gelatin mixture. Turn into mold on top of just-set layer. Chill several hours until firm. Unmold onto serving plate; garnish with crisp greens or cooked young green beans, if desired. Makes 4 luncheon servings. Arithmetic:

    12 ounces turkey = 3 lunches
    1 ounce Swiss cheese = ½ lunch
    ½ cup Sour Cream W.W. (⅓ cup cottage cheese = ½ lunch)

ROAST TURKEY

Roast the *turkey uncovered in a slow oven 300°F. until tender, allowing 25 minutes a pound under 12 pounds; 20 minutes a pound for larger turkey. Baste it every half hour or so with diced unlimited vegetables cooked in seasoned water. (Celery, green pepper and mushrooms seasoned with salt, pepper and onion flakes make a good baste.)

ROAST TURKEY HASH

> *1 pound roast turkey (white meat)
> ½ cup celery
> 1 green pepper
> 2 tablespoons Creole Sauce (see index for recipe)
> Worcestershire sauce
> *2 tablespoons nonfat dry milk solids
> Salt and freshly ground pepper

Weigh turkey. Put through meat grinder with celery and green pepper. Moisten with Creole Sauce, Worcestershire sauce and skim milk, and season with salt and pepper. Put into shallow casserole and bake at 350°F. without cover until top is crusty and brown. Serve with Creole or Tomato Sauce. Dinner for two.

Unlimited Vegetables

Salads! There are as many different kinds as there are greens in a vegetable garden. Of course you know about Boston lettuce, Iceberg, romaine, Bibb, chicory, endive, but have you tried the tiny florets of raw cauliflower, well-washed spinach leaves with the tough ribs removed, celery tops, grated cabbage, the little used Chinese cabbage, and green herbs? A wonderful collection of leaves which promote good nutrition.

143

You may eat all you want of the following vegetables:

asparagus	escarole	pimentos
beet greens	green and red pepper	radishes
broccoli	kohlrabi	rhubarb
cabbage	lettuce	sauerkraut
cauliflower	mung bean sprouts	spinach
celery	mushrooms	squash (green)
Chinese cabbage	mustard greens	string beans
cucumber	parsley	(French style)
endive	pickles	water cress

In the days when I was a size 20, it never occurred to me that vegetables could be delicious and satisfying. For the last few years, however, I have learned to enjoy vegetables when properly cooked. Yes, I think occasionally of high-caloried potatoes and pasta—which are not really vegetables, you know—but I think even more of the high-powered "sweet-talk" which I hear now that I am a size 12.

ALL-GREEN SALAD

Cold string beans mixed with Celery Sauce or Quick Tangy Dressing (see index for recipes) are all the ingredients you need for a salad course. Don't forget the bed of water cress.

ANOTHER DELICIOUS SALAD

Take any kind of green, washed and dried thoroughly in a towel, and refrigerated. Add white mushrooms (mushrooms which are not white can be peeled), sliced thin. Now a few young spinach leaves, ribs removed, washed and dried. Some crisply cooked young string beans. Blender Basil Dressing or Tomato French Dressing (see index for recipe). Put them all together and they spell—m-m-m-m! And unlimited too.

SALAD BOUQUET

1 package (10 ounces) frozen asparagus spears
6 tablespoons Tomato French Dressing (see index
    for recipe)
3 small stalks Belgian endive
½ head Boston lettuce

Cook asparagus, following label directions; drain. Place in a pie
plate; drizzle dressing over; chill at least 30 minutes to season. When
ready to serve, split each stalk of endive in half lengthwise; separate lettuce leaves. Place half an endive and 2 lettuce leaves on each
of 6 salad plates; arrange asparagus at sides. Drizzle any remaining
dressing in pie plate over all. Garnish with water cress, if you wish.
Six servings.

PERFECTION SALAD

1 tablespoon unflavored gelatin
½ cup cold water
1 cup sauerkraut juice, lemon juice and water
    combined
1 cup canned sauerkraut, drained
½ cup diced celery
1 tablespoon grated onion
1 diced pimento (or 2 tablespoons finely diced
    green or red pepper)

Sprinkle gelatin into small saucepan holding the cold water. Place
over low heat and stir to dissolve gelatin. Add sauerkraut juice,
lemon juice and water mixture. Chill to let thicken slightly (to consistency of unbeaten egg whites). Cut up drained sauerkraut into
small pieces. Add celery, grated onion, pimento (or pepper). Combine with gelatin mixture, turn into small mold and chill several

hours until firm. Unmold. Serve plain or with Tomato French Dressing (see index) to which you add horseradish sauce (about 1 teaspoon or to taste). Garnish with cucumber slices.

"POPCORN BOWL" W.W.

Cut into small pieces—green pepper, celery, cucumber, radishes, cauliflower, mushrooms (raw or canned)—as much as desired. Add to this one or two *fruits that you have left from daily supply. Nibble to your heart's content.

RAW VEGETABLE SALAD

Combine equal amounts of the following washed vegetables, all raw: spinach (hard rib removed), 2 varieties of lettuce, cut up, cauliflower (cut or finely chopped), sliced cucumbers, and sliced mushrooms. Marinate for half an hour in Tomato French Dressing W.W. and serve chilled. A good company salad. Unlimited.

TOSSED GREEN SALAD

½ head chicory
½ head romaine
1 head Boston lettuce
¼ head escarole
Leaves of fresh green spinach (remove heavy rib)

Wash greens well in advance. Drain and dry greens. Refrigerate wrapped in towel. When ready to use tear greens with hands into bite-size pieces and toss in a large bowl with a good Weight Watchers salad dressing.

VEGETABLE MELANGE

Cook 1 cup shredded washed cabbage with *⅓ cup tomato juice, liquid sugar substitute to taste, salt, pepper and garlic. After 10 minutes, add cooked mushrooms, celery, green or red peppers, bean sprouts.

THREE-LAYERED VEGETABLE SALAD

 3 envelopes unflavored gelatin
 2 teaspoons granulated sugar substitute
 ½ teaspoon salt
 1½ cups water
 ½ cup lemon juice
 ½ cup vinegar
 2½ cups water
 1 cup shredded green pepper
 1 cup sliced red radishes (unpeeled)
 1 cup shredded cabbage

Combine gelatin, sugar substitute, and salt in saucepan; add 1½ cups water. Stir over low heat until gelatin mixture is dissolved. Stir in lemon juice, vinegar, and 2½ cups water. Divide into three parts; chill each third one at a time until syrupy. Fold green pepper into one third. Spoon into 1½ quart mold; chill until almost set. Fold radishes into second third; spoon carefuly over green pepper layer; chill until almost set. Fold cabbage into remaining third; spoon carefully over radish layer. Chill several hours or until firm. Unmold onto serving plate; garnish with crisp greens. This will give you an evenly striped salad. Makes 6 servings.

Happiness is a good movie on T.V. and a bowl of Weight Watchers "Popcorn" (p. 146).

* *Limited food—see Menu Plan, p. 18-20, for legal amount.*

VEGETABLE SALAD BOWL

On a large flat tray lined with lettuce make separate mounds of chilled cooked green beans, cooked cauliflowerets, celery sticks, sliced raw mushrooms, asparagus tips, and *quarters of one tomato. Separate each mound with strips of pimento. Set a bowlful of Tomato French Dressing W.W. in the center of the tray. Serve at dinner.

Note: You may replace fresh tomato with cut-up cubes of Tomato Aspic (see index for recipe), and use another limited vegetable.

FRESH ASPARAGUS

Allow ½ pound or more per serving. Break off the tough ends—they will break at exactly the right spot. Stand stalks upright (tips at the top) in a deep kettle (bottle sterilizer is perfect) or lay flat in a large skillet. In either case, add 1 cup boiling water and cook, covered, until stalks are tender, about 12 minutes. Drain and save the liquid to use as stock. Serve the vegetables hot, or cover them with a vinaigrette sauce and let them marinate before serving.

ASPARAGUS BOUILLON

> 2 pounds fresh asparagus
> 2 quarts cold water
> Generous amount onion salt or dehydrated onion
>   flakes
> 2 sprigs parsley

Put all ingredients into a large kettle and let cook uncovered for 1 hour. Strain the soup, pressing out all the juices from the vegetables which are then discarded. Reheat gently. Serve over cut-up asparagus tips which have been cut into soup bowls.

Note: Liquid from canned asparagus tips can be used to replace an equal amount of water in recipe above.

ASPARAGUS BISQUE IN A BLENDER

Add an envelope of instant chicken or beef broth mix to the liquid and stalk ends left from cooking asparagus. Put into blender and let whirl at high speed until stalks are very fine. Heat, add *skim milk to taste, and serve at once. Measure skim milk used and add in daily total.

HERBAL ASPARAGUS SOUP

1. Put canned asparagus and liquid packed with it into a blender and purée it at high speed. Combine with an equal amount of chicken stock (may be made with instant chicken broth mix and hot water). Season with salt and pepper, a dash of grated onion or onion powder and a teaspoon of finely cut fresh tarragon, if available. Heat and serve, or store in refrigerator, reheating gently when ready to serve.

2. Ginger, nutmeg and curry are also extra-special seasoning for the soup. Don't let me forget parsley—lots of parsley whizzed up in the blender with the asparagus. There can't be too much of a good thing, at least in this case.

3. At other times, I have added a dash each of dried thyme, dried marjoram, cayenne pepper and a bay leaf (which should be removed before the soup is served). Chopped stalks of celery can also be simmered in water but then it takes longer.

For a winter bridge-group lunch, keep soup simmering in an electric skillet set on a tray. A collection of mugs and a soup ladle will permit the girls to help themselves as they come in. Just be sure to announce that the soup is a non-fattening type.

Lettuce, green beans, pea pods, and water cress make good additions to asparagus soup—in fact they are good in any soup.

If you like soup...you'll love this one!

CREAM OF ASPARAGUS AND MUSHROOM SOUP

Heat equal amounts of mushroom and asparagus bouillon. To the resulting bouillon add *nonfat dry milk powder to taste. Season with salt and crushed red pepper. Heat in double boiler or over low flame so milk does not boil. Serves 4.

Note: The nonfat dry milk solids must be counted in day's allowance of milk. One-third cup of powder is the equivalent of 1 cup skim milk.

ASPARAGUS ASPIC

        1 tablespoon unflavored gelatin
        1½ cups vegetable liquid or water
        3 tablespoons vinegar
        1 teaspoon salt
        ⅛ teaspoon sugar substitute
        1 cup cut-up asparagus tips
        1 tablespoon chopped parsley
        1 tablespoon finely diced celery
        ¼ cup diced pimento
        ½ teaspoon freshly ground pepper

Sprinkle 1 envelope plain gelatin on ½ cup water or liquid left from cooking vegetables. Place over low heat and stir to dissolve gelatin. Add remaining ingredients. Stir well. Put into wet mold and chill several hours. Unmold and serve.

ASPARAGUS VINAIGRETTE

> 2 cups tarragon vinegar
> ¼ cup finely minced parsley
> Few drops lemon juice
> 1 teaspoon onion juice (made by scraping top of
>   cut onion)
> Several cut-up capers
> Cooked asparagus

Cook tarragon vinegar until it is reduced by half (about 20 minutes). Add finely minced parsley, lemon juice, onion juice and capers. Mix together and pour over cooked asparagus. Then chill both and serve very cold. This same sauce can be served over any vegetable.

ASPARAGUS AU GRATIN ON TOAST

> *2 ounces grated hard cheese
> Dash of paprika
> 6 stalks cooked asparagus (or more
>   if you wish)

For each luncheon serving, sprinkle grated hard cheese and a dash of paprika over cooked asparagus. Put into 350° F. oven until cheese melts. Serve with toast points (1 slice of white bread, toasted and cut into four triangles).

Note: The asparagus is unlimited, so you are at liberty to increase the amount if you so desire.

* *Limited food—see Menu Plan, p. 18-20, for legal amount.*

BEAN SPROUTS

Wash canned bean sprouts. Heat with 1 tablespoon soy sauce and ¼ teaspoon salt. Cover and heat slowly for 5 minutes, then take off cover and stir for 1 minute longer. Serve hot or cold.

BEAN-SPROUT SOUP

    1 envelope or cube for chicken
      or beef broth
    1 cup water
    ½ cup bean sprouts or
      more if desired

Heat the water, add the powder or cube for broth, and washed, drained bean sprouts. Heat and serve—an unlimited soup.

LEMON BROCCOLI

    1 bunch broccoli
    1 tablespoon lemon juice
    1 tablespoon water
    Dash of sugar substitute—granulated,
      liquid or tablet

Trim away outer leaves and tough ends of broccoli. Slice thick stalks into 1-inch pieces and put in bottom of saucepan, with flowerettes on top. Barely cover with boiling salted water and cook 10 minutes until they are just tender. Drain and put into heated serving bowl. Mix lemon juice with the equivalent of 1 teaspoon sugar. Drizzle over cooked broccoli. 4 servings.

SKILLET CABBAGE

> ¼ head small cabbage
> ¼ cup water
> Salt and pepper to taste
> Liquid sugar substitute

Soak cabbage in salted cold water for 20 minutes to clean it. Shred as for cole slaw. Boil water in skillet and add cabbage, salt and pepper. Cover and cook until tender, watching to be sure it does not burn. Shredded cabbage cooks very quickly. Season to taste with liquid sugar substitute.

SWEET AND SOUR CABBAGE

Simmer cut-up cabbage in 1 cup *tomato juice, with sweetened sugar substitute.

COLE SLAW

Soak cabbage in salted water for ½ hour, then drain it. Shred enough (about ½ head) to make 3 cups. Combine with 3 table-spoons diced celery, 3 tablespoons diced green pepper and 3 table-spoons diced pimentos. Mix with Mustard Dressing W.W. (see index for recipe and use full amount). Refrigerate at least ½ hour before serving.

You can thicken broth by adding puréed cooked vegetables or by reheating it with raw vegetables put through blender.

CABBAGE SOUP

2 cups celery, cut up (including green tops)
1½ tablespoons dehydrated onion flakes
2 quarts water
4 cups cabbage, shredded
2 tablespoons lemon juice
2 teaspoons liquid sugar substitute
*2 cups tomato juice
6 peppercorns
2 envelopes powdered chicken broth
2 tablespoons salt, or to taste

Cook celery and onion in water. Mash them through a strainer, extracting all juices. Add juices to cabbage and lemon juice. Cook for 1 hour. Stir in sugar substitute, tomato juice, peppercorns, and chicken broth. Cook 1 hour longer. Season with salt. Four servings.

RED CABBAGE

Add a little vinegar while cooking red cabbage so it will keep its bright red color. Otherwise, it turns an unattractive purple. Cook it for about 30 minutes. Caraway seeds add interesting flavor to red cabbage.

RED CABBAGE RELISH

Finely shred 1 head of red cabbage into a large bowl. Cover with salt and let stand 30 minutes. Squeeze the cabbage dry (between your hands), put the leaves into a bowl, add a teaspoon of sugar substitute and mix well. Slowly stir in wine vinegar, a bit at a time, mixing well. Serve as relish.

RED CABBAGE SALAD

Slice uncooked red cabbage very thin and soak in salted water. Put in a salad bowl, season with salt and pepper. Serve with Garlic Tomato Juice Dressing.

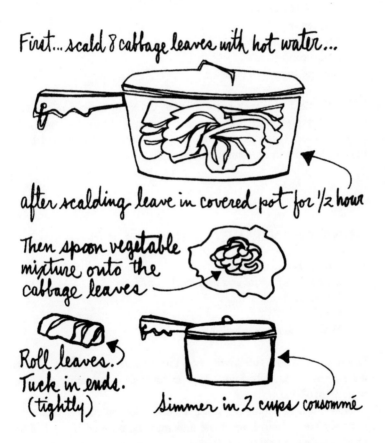

First... scald 8 cabbage leaves with hot water...

after scalding leave in covered pot for ½ hour

Then spoon vegetable mixture onto the cabbage leaves

Roll leaves.
Tuck in ends.
(tightly)

Simmer in 2 cups consommé

* Limited food—see Menu Plan, p. 18-20, for legal amount.

CABBAGE STUFFED WITH VEGETABLES

>8 cabbage leaves
>1 cup French-style green beans
>3 teaspoons dehydrated onion flakes, barely
>   covered with tomato juice to moisten
>2 stalks celery
>½ cup bean sprouts
>½ green pepper
>1 teaspoon chopped parsley
>2 cups consommé
>Salt and pepper to taste

Scald cabbage leaves with boiling water and leave covered in pot for ½ hour. Chop all vegetables fine, add parsley and mix with salt and pepper. Spoon vegetable mixture onto each leaf. Roll tight and tuck in ends. Simmer in consommé 1 hour.

HUNGARIAN SAUERKRAUT

>1-pound can sauerkraut
>*2 cups tomato juice and beef stock combined
>Dehydrated onion flakes
>Paprika
>½ teaspoon sugar substitute

Drain liquid from sauerkraut, add tomatoes and beef stock, onion flakes, and sugar substitute. Bake uncovered in casserole for one hour at 350° F.

Note: Whole *tomatoes make a good addition to this casserole, but they are a limited vegetable and must be counted if used. One tomato makes one serving at dinner.

* *Limited food—see Menu Plan, p. 18-20, for legal amount.*

MOCK POTATO PUDDING— BAKED CAULIFLOWER

Whip cooked cauliflower (it should be slightly mushy) with liquid left from cooking it or with *skim milk. (If cauliflower is too cold to whip, heat in milk or water.) Season to taste with salt, pepper, and onion flakes or juice of onion. Bake in individual casseroles.

CAULIFLOWER AND GREEN BEAN SALAD

Buy a large white cauliflower. Separate into flowerettes and soak in salted water for half an hour. Then cook covered in 3 inches of boiling salted water for 12 minutes, or until tender but not mushy. Drain and set aside.

Break off the stem ends of young green beans, wash and put into covered saucepan with boiling salted water. Cook about 20 minutes, then drain and cool.

Combine cool cauliflower and string beans in a bowl. Sprinkle with ¼ cup cut-up parsley sprigs from which you removed tough stems. Cover with Tomato French Dressing W.W. (see index for recipe). Let marinate about half an hour. Serve in lettuce cups.

CAULIFLOWER CHEDDAR

    1 small head of cauliflower, cooked
  *4 ounces grated cheddar cheese
    Salt and pepper
    Paprika

Place a cooked (but still white) head of cauliflower in a round baking dish. Sprinkle grated cheese over it, season with salt and pepper, and paprika if you wish. Place in moderately hot oven just long enough to melt cheese. Serve in baking dish. An easily made attractive luncheon main dish for two (each portion: 2 ounces cheese). The cauliflower can be cooked the day ahead, and heated in the oven with 2 ounces grated hard cheese, to make an individual serving. The little flowers of the cauliflower, uncooked and washed, make a good addition to the salad bowl. Serve with Blender Lemon-Parsley Sauce.

CELERY

Cut celery stalks crosswise into 1-inch pieces. Place in saucepan, sprinkle with 1 packet instant broth mix and 1 teaspoon onion flakes. Add boiling water to cover and cook 15-20 minutes until celery is tender. Most of the water should be boiled down. If not, cook uncovered on high heat, shaking pan to be sure it does not burn.

CELERY BRAISED IN ORANGE JUICE

Cut a bunch of celery into large pieces. Place in heavy pan with *2 ounces orange juice. Cook until tender.

Note: Orange juice must be counted; two ounces equals one-half fruit.

CELERY SOUP

    4-5 stalks celery, leaves included, cut in
      1-inch pieces
    3 cups water
    2 envelopes instant broth mix
  *2 teaspoons nonfat dry milk

Cook celery until soft. Add broth mix. Pour into blender. Add milk and blend 10-15 seconds. Reheat and serve.

CELERY VINAIGRETTE

Sprinkle cooked celery with Tomato Sauce (see index), spiked with vinegar or lemon juice, salt, freshly grated pepper and chopped chives. Refrigerate and serve cold. Tarragon vinegar is a tangy marinade for cooked celery—let it stand overnight.

CELERY HORS D'OEUVRE

Arrange cooked celery sticks on a shallow plate. Make a small cross of pimento strips on each stick. Cooked celery may also be sprinkled lightly with vinegar, lemon or *tomato juice, salt, freshly grated pepper, and chopped chives (total about ¼ cup). Refrigerate. Serve cold.

Festive Looking!

Cooked celery stalks.
Make small cross with pimento strips.
serve cold!

CUCUMBER SALAD

Slice peeled cucumbers very thin. Place in bowl. Salt thoroughly, cover bowl and refrigerate overnight. Next day pour off water. Add ¼ cup of vinegar and 2 teaspoons of liquid sugar substitute; serve after 1 hour.

WILTED CUCUMBERS

  3 large cucumbers
  Coarse salt
  Freshly grated pepper
  ⅓ cup vinegar
  Water
  ⅛ teaspoon sugar substitute

Peel cucumbers and score by making tracks lengthwise with a fork. Slice thin. Arrange in layers in a bowl, salting each layer generously. Let wilt in refrigerator for several hours. Press out salt water that forms. Grate pepper over slices. Combine vinegar and enough water to total ½ cup. Sweeten with sugar substitute. Pour over cucumbers and let marinate in refrigerator 1 hour. Serves 6. Unlimited.

CHILLED CHICKEN CONSOMME AND CUCUMBER REFRESHER

  4 cups consommé
  1 cup shredded, pared cucumber
  ½ teaspoon dill weed

Remove fat from soup. Combine soup, water, and cucumber. Chill. Sprinkle each serving with dill weed. Makes 6 servings.

DILLED CUCUMBER SLICES

    2 or 3 large cucumbers
  *1 cup buttermilk
    4 sprigs fresh dill
    Salt

Peel and dice cucumbers. Snip dill into buttermilk and pour over
cucumber. Salt to taste. Allow to stand in refrigerator at least an
hour before serving. May be served at lunch or dinner. Buttermilk
used must be counted towards day's allowance of milk.

CUCUMBER RING

    2 tablespoons gelatin
    ½ cup cold water
    2 tablespoons lemon juice
    1½ cups chicken stock
    1 teaspoon grated onion, or dehydrated onion
        flakes, soaked in water to cover for 5 minutes
    1 stalk celery, cut up
    1 sprig parsley, minced
    1 teaspoon salt
    Dash cayenne pepper
    3 peeled cucumbers

Soak gelatin in cold water and lemon juice. Combine chicken stock,
onion, celery, parsley, salt and a dash of cayenne. Simmer for 20
minutes. Strain. Add gelatin and dissolve in hot stock. Grate peeled
cucumbers. Add to gelatin mixture. Pour into wet mold. Unmold on
water cress or lettuce.

  * *Limited food—see Menu Plan, p. 18-20, for legal amount.*

ESCAROLE SOUP

,   2 cups chicken, vegetable or beef bouillon (may
        be made with instant-broth mix)
   *1 tablespoon tomato juice
    1 cup shredded escarole
    Salt to taste

Bring stock to full boil. Add tomato juice and shredded escarole. Cook gently about 10 minutes. Serve at once. This is an unlimited quick soup that can be used at any desired time.

FRESH GREEN "STRING" BEANS

To make sure beans are young, break one in half and listen for the snap and crack that says beans are fresh and crisp—not dehydrated. Wash them in cold water and cut into long strips. Drop into pot holding about ¼ cup rapidly boiling salted water. Cover and let boil until beans are tender but still bright green—they turn brownish-green when overcooked. Salt may be added before serving. A teaspoon of dill seed added in the last 3 minutes gives good flavor. Enjoy them hot or serve cold, alone or combined with other vegetables. They are an important item in the Weight Watchers menu.

Note: Once upon a time, when beans had strings on them, they were called string beans. The strings had long since been bred out of them, but many people still know them by the old name. We use the names interchangeably throughout this book.

GREEN BEANS AND CELERY

    1 cup boiling water
    1 cup sliced celery
    1 teaspoon salt
    9 ounces frozen French-style green beans

Add boiling water to salt and celery in saucepan. As soon as water boils again, add green beans. Separate beans with a fork, cover and cook until greens are tender but still green—8 minutes. (Celery takes longer to cook than beans, so start it cooking first.)

FRESH STRING BEANS AND MUSHROOMS ORIENTALE

    1 pound fresh young green beans
    1 pound fresh mushrooms, washed quickly
    ½ teaspoon salt
    ¼ teaspoon pepper
    1 tablespoon soy sauce
    2 tablespoons water
    ½ teaspoon MSG

Buy small young beans, as these are the ones used for French-style string beans, permitted in unlimited quantities. Wash them, discarding tips. Cut off hard end of stems from mushrooms and slice mushrooms. Place in heavy skillet. Add rest of ingredients. Simmer gently until most of liquid has boiled away. Stir occasionally.

COLD STRING BEAN STEW (Loob-yee ib Zayt)

    2 packages frozen French-style green beans
    *2 onions
    1 cup chicken stock
    *2 tomatoes
    1 teaspoon salt
    ½ teaspoon whole peppercorns

Wash and drain string beans and set aside. Peel and halve onions, and slice down from stem into slivers. Put chicken stock in large heavy kettle, add onions, and cook until onions are soft. Add string beans, cover, and cook for 30 minutes, adding a few tablespoons of chicken stock as necessary to keep beans from burning. Turn them often. Add tomatoes. Sprinkle in salt and crushed peppercorns, and cook for final 30 minutes. Most of the liquid should now have evaporated—if it has not, remove cover and cook for another few minutes. Serve cold. The onions and tomatoes are limited vegetables. Therefore this stew must serve 4 portions at dinner.

SPANISH STRING BEANS

    2 diced pimentos
    ¼ teaspoon dry onion flakes
  *2 tablespoons skim milk solids
    ½ cup chicken stock
    9-ounce package frozen French-style green beans

Simmer pimentos, onion flakes and skim milk in chicken stock for 10 minutes. Add frozen green beans, cover and cook until beans are done (10-12 minutes). Do not overcook beans. Unlimited vegetable, but count milk.

MOCK SPLIT-PEA SOUP

    3 cups water
  *1 carrot
    2 celery stalks
    6 sprigs parsley
  *1 onion
    2 cups French-style green beans (#303 can)
    1½ cups cooked asparagus
    Dash of mace
    1 bay leaf
    ½ teaspoon salt

Combine in soup kettle and cook for ¾ hour water, carrot, celery, celery stalks, parsley and onion. Purée in blender or pour through strainer, mashing the vegetables with a spoon to extract all the liquid and flavor. Put purée back in kettle. Add string beans and asparagus, including liquid, mace, and bay leaf. Let simmer ½ hour or more. Discard bay leaf and serve hot. Delicious! Serves 4 at dinner.

Note: To use this as an unlimited soup, omit carrots and onion. Add onion flakes for seasoning.

CURRIED CREAM OF KALE SOUP

Kale, a member of the cabbage family, is unlimited, but so was my distaste for it—that is, until I developed this recipe.

- 10 ounces frozen kale, cooked according to directions on package, or 2 cups cooked fresh kale
- 2 envelopes instant chicken broth mix
- 2 cups hot water
- 1 teaspoon curry powder
- *⅔ cup nonfat dry milk solids

Place in blender container in two batches and blend until kale is very fine, then turn into saucepan and heat. Makes 6 servings. Reduce daily milk allowance by ⅓ cup for each serving. To use as unlimited soup, omit skim milk and use only ¾ teaspoon curry powder.

SALAD PIMENTADE

Just a simple salad of French-style green beans which have been cooked only until done, then garnished with strips of pimento . . . and now you have the salad with the fancy name.

* *Limited food—see Menu Plan, p. 18-20, for legal amount.*

MUSHROOMS

Mushrooms, an unlimited vegetable, are a mainstay of the W.W. program. If you have bought more than you can use quickly (they cannot be kept too long), wash them, separate stems from caps and cook for 3 or 4 minutes in a little bit of salted water and lemon juice (the latter to prevent them from darkening). Store the mushrooms in the refrigerator and use in any of the recipes. The caps can be stuffed, the stems ground or sliced and served over meat or fish and the liquid used in soups.

Mushrooms combine well with almost all other vegetables, and are frequently used in combination, filled, as part of a sauce, etc.

Store this one in refrigerator. Use as needed!

Sprinkle vegetables with COARSE salt. Do not add water. Cook until you have desired tenderness. (We like them crisp) Prevent scorching... turn often!

MUSHROOM "MYCHELE"

> Celery (cut long way)
> Green or red peppers (cut long way)
> Fresh mushrooms
> Bean sprouts

Sprinkle vegetables with coarse salt—no water. Use any desired flavor—perhaps a garlic clove, pressed to extract the juices. Cook as
you like it—I like it when the vegetables are crisp—in a heavy saucepan or large skillet. Turn as necessary to prevent scorching. Store
in refrigerator and use as needed. Other unlimited vegetables can
be added. Use as snack, as vegetable, etc.

MUSHROOM HORS D'OEUVRE

Cook mushroom caps at high heat in ¼ cup beef stock; season
with salt and pepper and let them steam for about 1 minute. Remove
from heat while they are still firm and place them on a bed of
parsley or water cress, set as a border on a round tray. In the middle
of the tray put a bowl holding Sour Cream W.W. (made with
*⅔ cup cottage cheese and water). Surround with celery rings or
sticks. Provide small spoons so guests can fill caps with sour cream.

Note: The mushrooms are unlimited but the cottage cheese (in the
sour cream) must be counted. This is a very good party luncheon
dish.

BROILED MUSHROOMS

Mushrooms need 6-8 minutes under the broiler. They do not need
turning. Season the caps with salt and pepper and broil hollow side
up (the hollow will hold the juices which gather).

CREAMED MUSHROOM SAUCE

    1 cup sliced mushrooms (packed tight)
    1 envelope instant chicken-broth mix
    ¼ cup water
   *2 tablespoons nonfat dry milk powder

Select firm white mushrooms and wash them quickly. Cut them lengthwise, so that each slice has some cap and stem. Put into heavy small saucepan, with an envelope of chicken-broth mix and water. Cover (if saucepan doesn't have a cover, use aluminum foil). Cook 5 minutes, stir in milk and turn off heat. This is a highly seasoned sauce, excellent over chicken, fish, or vegetables. It may be used at any time, and is excellent on a slice of toast, or over hard-cooked eggs, at luncheon. The milk powder must be counted as ⅓ cup skim milk; everything else is unlimited.

MUSHROOM AND PARSLEY SAUCE

Make Creamed Mushroom Sauce and add chopped parsley after heat is turned off. (I happen to prefer the fresh uncooked parsley flavor in this dish.) Don't be stingy with parsley—it's legal, it's unlimited, it's good, and it has a real affinity for mushrooms.

DEVILED MUSHROOMS EN CASSEROLE

1 pound fresh mushrooms
1 green pepper
1 teaspoon onion juice (scraped from cut onion)
Salt
Pepper
Dash of chili powder
1-2 tablespoons lemon juice

Wash fresh mushrooms and discard a thin slice of stem. Put through coarse blade of food chopper with green pepper into mixing bowl. Season to taste with onion, salt, pepper, and chili powder. Add enough lemon juice to make smooth paste. Press paste to bottom and sides of a shallow casserole and use in any of the following ways:
  1. Drop an egg in center of casserole and sprinkle top with fine

*crumbs (made from bread crusts left from slice of allowed bread.) Bake for 20 minutes in 350°F. oven (moderate). Serve hot, maybe for Sunday breakfast?

2. For luncheon, grate 2 ounces of hard *cheese into casserole, moisten with *tomato juice, and add fine *crumbs (made from ½ slice luncheon bread whizzed in blender). Heat about 10 minutes in moderate oven until cheese is melted.

3. Use as filling for stuffed mushrooms. Bake 10 minutes in moderate (350°F.) oven. Enough for about 6 servings.

MUSHROOM PUREE

1 pound mushrooms
2 tablespoons lemon juice
1 tablespoon caraway seeds
3 tablespoons dehydrated onion flakes
Chives
1 teaspoon coarse salt
½ teaspoon grated pepper

Remove the stems from mushrooms and peel the caps. Sprinkle lemon juice over the caps so they stay white and set them in the refrigerator. Wash stems and peelings and put into a pot with 1 quart water, caraway seeds and onion. Let cook over moderate flame for 1 hour. Turn off heat and let the flavors blend for half a day or overnight. Then put the stock back to cook some more, but this time add the chives and salt and pepper. Put everything into blender and blend until you have a purée. Store in refrigerator.

There are many ways to serve this purée. Combine with *tomato, spinach or *skim milk and heat to serve as soup. Combine purée with beaten *egg yolk, fold in with beaten *egg white and make soufflé in small casserole. Best of all, serve hot purée over sliced raw mushroom caps for luncheon bouillon.

* *Limited food—see Menu Plan, p. 18-20, for legal amount.*

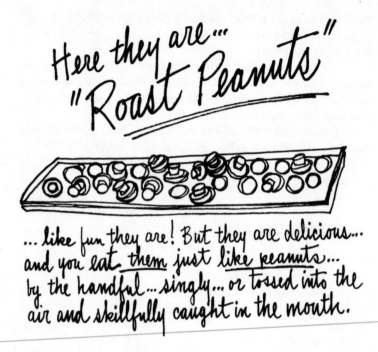

Here they are...
"Roast Peanuts"

... like fun they are! But they are delicious...
and you eat them just like peanuts...
by the handful... singly... or tossed into the
air and skillfully caught in the mouth.

"ROAST PEANUTS"

> Canned button mushrooms
> Salt

You didn't *really* think you could eat peanuts, did you? These are good, too, but in a very different way. Drain all liquid from can (use this liquid in one of the other mushroom recipes). Spread mushrooms evenly on cookie tin or aluminum foil tray. Sprinkle generously with salt. Bake in slow oven, 250° F., about 1 hour or until mushrooms are brown and completely dry. These taste very much like peanuts and can be eaten whenever desired. Mushrooms may also be broiled under low flame, as far from the heat as possible, turning as necessary. Watch to be sure that mushrooms don't burn. Once you've tasted them, you'll know why I call them peanuts, at least, I hope you will know!

MUSHROOM STUFFED WITH SPINACH

Cook 10 ounces packaged spinach, drain, and purée in blender or in food mill. Set aside. Quickly wash 18 large mushrooms. Remove stems, cover with chicken stock, cook 10 minutes, chop and reserve them. Sprinkle caps with lemon juice. Combine cooked stems, puréed spinach, ¾ teaspoon salt, ¼ teaspoon pepper, 1 crushed clove garlic, generous amount of onion seasoning or flakes, dash dry mustard and ¼ teaspoon nutmeg. Fill mushroom caps with mixture. Bake 15 minutes in shallow pan at 375° F. or freeze and use as desired. Unlimited.

BLACK MUSHROOM SOUP

8 Chinese black mushrooms
4 cups clear beef broth
Cut-up chives

Cook the mushrooms for 10 minutes until soft. (Save cooking liquid to use as base for sauce, etc.) Slice the cooked mushrooms and heat with the beef consommé. Serve with cut-up chives as garnish. 4 servings.

PIQUANT MUSHROOMS

Quickly wash 1 pound mushrooms. Discard rough ends and separate stems from caps. Put the caps in a shallow baking dish, flat side up. Chop the stems, sprinkle with 1 tablespoon lemon juice, add 1 tablespoon each of finely chopped parsley, chives, green pepper, and grated onion. Sprinkle lightly with salt, pepper and nutmeg. Add ¾ cup hot water in which you dissolved 1 envelope instant chicken broth mix. Bake as part of an oven meal or separately for about 20 minutes in a moderate oven (350°F.). (At luncheon, serve with a slice of toast lightly brushed with cut clove of garlic.)

* *Limited food—see Menu Plan, p. 18-20, for legal amount.*

TURKISH PEPPERS

1 pound frying peppers
¼ cup chicken stock
Salt

Brown strips of frying pepper in a hot dry skillet. As soon as skin begins to blister add chicken stock, and cook peppers until done. Refrigerate.

VARIATION:

Add salt to *Sour Cream W.W. and serve with chilled peppers as salad.

PEPPER JAM

Drain a 7-ounce can of pimentos and force through food chopper into a saucepan. Add 1 tablespoon sugar substitute and ½ cup vinegar. Let boil, stirring gently until mixture is consistency of jam (220° F. on thermometer). Pour into small sterilized glasses and when cool cover with melted paraffin. You can use 3 sweet red peppers instead of pimentos. Remove seeds and membrane, put through food chopper, sprinkle with salt and let stand 3-4 hours. Drain, rinse and use as above.

PEPPERS AND PIMENTO

Green and red peppers (also called bell peppers) can be eaten to your heart's content. They make good containers for other foods. Large peppers may be cut in half lengthwise, seeds and membranes discarded, and used uncooked to hold salads or salad dips. Let cook gently for 5 minutes in water to cover if peppers are to be used as cases for hot foods.

Pimentos, Spanish for pepper, are sold roasted as well as in vinegar brine.

Pieces of pimento shaped into cups held with toothpicks can be filled with dill pickle relish and served as a garnish for a fish platter. And a few slices of lemon set on the platter will complete the ensemble to suit the eye of the most critical artist.

FILLING FOR PEPPERS

Cooked *chicken and mushrooms put through a food grinder, moistened with beef stock and seasoned with salt and pepper makes a good filling for steamed peppers. Heat in hot oven.

CHILES RELLENAS (Stuffed Peppers Mexican Style)

*1 ounce hard cheese
  3 roasted pimentos
*1 egg, separated
  1 tablespoon water
*1 slice bread
*1 cup tomato juice
  1 clove garlic, slightly crushed
  Dash of oregano or cayenne pepper

Cut hard cheese into 3 strips. Wrap each strip in a roasted pimento. Secure with toothpick. Combine 1 egg yolk with water, fold in egg white, stiffly beaten. Add ½ cup bread crumbs (made from luncheon slice of bread, whizzed in blender). Dip pimentos into this fluffy batter and refrigerate so batter sets. Heat tomato juice in skillet or shallow pan, add crushed clove of garlic and a dash of oregano or hot cayenne pepper if you prefer. As soon as juice is heated, transfer the cheese-stuffed pimentos to pan with a spoon. Any batter that dripped off the pimentos can be spooned in also. Cook about 10 minutes until cheese is melted, remove garlic, and transfer sauce and pimentos to plate. Makes an excellent luncheon dish; can be made in double quantity and reheated.

STUFFED PEPPERS

    4 large peppers
    Radishes, cut up
    Kohlrabi, cut up
    Chopped chives, minced
    Cucumbers, diced
    Fennel or celery, diced

Cut thin stem tops from 4 plump peppers, red and green mixed. Remove seeds. Make a stuffing of the other vegetables. Mix with Sauce Chambord or Tomato French Dressing. Sprinkle top with chopped parsley.

RHUBARB

    5 pounds raw rhubarb
    ¼ cup water
    Few drops red food coloring (optional)
    1 capful lemon extract
    7 level teaspoons sugar substitute or to taste

Trim leaves at top of rhubarb and wash. Then cut into 1-inch pieces. Put into large pot with water. Use small flame and watch carefully. Cover. Stir occasionally until desired consistency, about 20 minutes. Remove from heat (add red coloring if desired). Add lemon extract and sugar substitute. Chill and serve cold. It will thicken as it cools. Free food—eat and enjoy.

ROSY RED RHUBARB

Cut rhubarb into 1-inch pieces and sprinkle with noncaloric carbonated drink—black cherry or grape, or make your own choice. Bake in slow oven 300° F., until done. Unlimited.

CHILLED SPICED RHUBARB

Here's a dessert that's in tune with spring . . . Chilled Spiced Rhubarb. Sweet and lively in flavor, this refreshing dessert is thrifty and quick to make.

1½ pounds rhubarb, washed
½ cup water
½ cup vinegar
½ teaspoon ginger
½ teaspoon cinnamon
¼ teaspoon cloves
4 tablespoons liquid sugar substitute

Cut rhubarb into 1-inch pieces. (Pink, tender rhubarb does not have to be peeled.) Place in a large saucepan with remaining ingredients. Cover and simmer for 20 to 25 minutes, or until rhubarb is tender. Chill before serving. Makes 8 servings.

STEWED RHUBARB

Rhubarb is considered a fruit in some areas and a vegetable in others. In this book, we classify it as a vegetable—and an unlimited one.

Wash and trim rhubarb. Tender stalks do not have to be peeled. Lay several stalks on a board, and slice them into pieces about 1 inch long. Put into a saucepan with a tablespoon or so of water for each pound of rhubarb, cover and cook gently for 5-10 minutes. Add sugar substitute (about 1 tablespoon, or to taste, for each pound). Serve hot or cold.

BAKED RHUBARB

Cut rhubarb into 1-inch pieces and sprinkle with lemon juice and grated lemon rind. Add sugar substitute. Bake at 300°F. (slow oven) until rhubarb is tender. This is an unlimited vegetable.

RHUBARB PUNCH

Wash 4 cups rhubarb and cut into 1-inch cubes. Add a minimum of water and cook in saucepan until tender. Stir in 1½ tablespoons granulated sugar substitute. Put into blender and purée at high speed until rhubarb is liquefied. When ready to serve pour over ice in punch bowl. Add 2 cups non-caloric ginger ale and 3 tablespoons lemon juice. Taste and add more sweetener if you think it needs it. Eight servings.

"SPAGHETTI"

    2 teaspoons dehydrated onion flakes
    1 clove garlic, minced
    Salt
    Pepper
   *12 ounces tomato juice
    1 teaspoon liquid sugar substitute
    Large can bean sprouts

Cook first 6 ingredients together to make a thick sauce (about 1 hour). Drain bean sprouts, clean in fresh water under faucet. Cook ½ hour, or until soft. Drain thoroughly. Pour sauce over sprouts.

SPINACH DELIGHT

    1 box frozen (whole leaf) spinach
    1 can bean sprouts
    1 can mushrooms (fresh if desired)

Cook spinach following package directions. Drain thoroughly. Drain can of bean sprouts, and combine with spinach. Add undrained can of mushrooms. Season well with salt, pepper, garlic powder, and onion powder; heat and serve.

* *Limited food—see Menu Plan, p. 18-20, for legal amount.*

SPINACH TIMBALES FOR LUNCH

    1¼ cups cooked spinach, chopped
    Salt and pepper to taste
    Few grains nutmeg
    1½ teaspoons prepared horseradish
*1 egg, beaten slightly
*½ cup skim milk

Combine all ingredients and pack into casserole. Bake in a pan of hot water in 350°F. oven for 1 hour or until knife inserted into center comes out clean. Unmold on platter. Serves 1. Good with Sauce Chambord and Mushrooms Stuffed with Tuna, using 2 ounces of fish.

CREAM OF SPINACH SOUP W.W.

*2 cups skim milk
  1 teaspoon salt
  Dash pepper
  ⅛ teaspoon nutmeg
  2 cups tightly packed young spinach
    or ½ cup drained cooked spinach

Place milk, salt, pepper, and nutmeg in glass container of blender. Add young spinach leaves (remove any tough ribs). Run until contents are puréed. Heat in saucepan, stirring constantly. Makes 4 servings. (For luncheon, bread crumbs made in blender from bread crust may be beaten with soup to thicken it.)

SPINACH AND ROMAINE SOUP

Cook cleaned spinach and cut-up romaine leaves in boiling salted water. Add 1 envelope chicken-broth mix. When romaine is tender

—about 10 minutes—put into blender with liquid, and add finely chopped chives and parsley. Purée. Serve chilled as summer soup, add *skim milk or *buttermilk if desired. If skim milk or buttermilk are added, they must be counted as part of day's allowance.

SPINACH SOUP (Unlimited)

> 10-ounce package fresh (or frozen) spinach
> 2 cups water
> 1½ teaspoon instant minced onion
> ¾ teaspoon salt
> Dash of freshly grated nutmeg
> 2 envelopes instant chicken broth mix

Using a blender. If spinach is fresh, clean and wash it and remove tough stems. Feed ⅓ of the spinach into blender with ¼ cup water. Cover, turn on blender and run until spinach is smooth. Pour into saucepan. Repeat until all of the spinach is blended. Add onion, salt, nutmeg, chicken mix and remaining water. Cook over moderate heat for 5 minutes. Pour into quart jar and refrigerate until ready to use. Cover jar loosely (do not cover until soup has cooled). Use as is, or dilute with equal parts of chicken stock.

Lacking a blender. Clean and wash spinach. Remove tough stems. Cook for 6 minutes in saucepan with no added water. Put through strainer or food mill or chop fine. Add remaining ingredients and cook over moderate heat for 5 minutes. Store as directed.

SPINACH SOUP WITH FINE HERBS

Follow recipe for Spinach Soup but *omit* nutmeg and add 2 tablespoons of combined fresh finely chopped parsley, chives and rosemary (or basil). Cook and serve as directed.

HOT SPINACH SALAD

1 pound fresh spinach
1 tablespoon lemon juice
3 tablespoons chicken broth
¼ teaspoon salt
¼ teaspoon Worcestershire sauce
Granulated, liquid, or tablet sugar substitute

Remove stems from spinach; wash leaves well; drain. Place in a large saucepan, without adding any water; cover. Steam 2 or 3 minutes, or just until leaves wilt; drain any liquid from pan. In a cup, combine lemon juice, broth, salt, Worcestershire sauce, and a dash of your favorite sweetener, using the equivalent of 1 teaspoon sugar. Pour over spinach; toss to coat leaves well. Four servings.

SPINACH WITH SOUR CREAM

Cook spinach with a little water until tender. Drain. Season with salt, pepper and nutmeg. Put on a salad plate. Add Sour Cream W.W. (see index for recipe) made with *⅓ cup cottage cheese and water. Slice *1 hard-cooked egg and arrange around spinach. Refrigerate to chill. Toast a *slice of bread, cut into 4 points, and arrange around platter. Luncheon for 1.

SPINACH STROGANOFF

Arrange a serving of cooked spinach on platter. Combine Sour Cream W.W. (made from *⅓ cup cottage cheese and water), 1 teaspoon onion juice (scrape a cut onion) and 2 tablespoons finely grated horseradish. Season with salt and pepper and serve over spinach. Serve with *Iced Tomato Juice, and an *Open-faced Sandwich made from 2 ounces of cooked white meat of chicken at luncheon.

TURNIP AND OTHER GREENS

Beet and turnip tops, dandelion greens, dark outside leaves of escarole and even the tops of radishes and carrots are useful in cooking. They should be thoroughly washed, a few pieces at a time, in several baths of lukewarm water, and lifted out of each bath so that the grit and sand are left behind. Cut the greens and cook in a minimum amount of water, or put through blender and use as health cocktail.

WATER-CRESS SOUP FOR ONE

Combine in blender and blend until smooth, about 1 minute: ¾ cup water, 1 chicken bouillon cube or envelope of instant chicken broth mix, and ¼ bunch water cress or firmly packed young spinach (remove hard rib). Heat to boiling point and serve immediately or chill.

HERBED ZUCCHINI

> 6 medium-size zucchini (about 1½ pounds)
> ½ teaspoon salt
> 1 teaspoon mixed salad herbs
> ½ cup water

Trim zucchini; halve each crosswise. Make 4 or 5 cuts in each half, starting at wide end and cutting almost to tip. Combine with salt, herbs, and water in a medium-size frying pan; cover. Cook 10 minutes, or until crisply tender; drain. Place on heated serving plates; spread cuts to form a fan. Makes 6 servings. (Salad herbs can be chopped parsley, chives, basil, rosemary, etc.)

VEGETABLE LUNCHEON PANCAKE

Follow recipe for Austrian Breakfast Pancake (see index for recipe) but top with well-drained unlimited vegetables. Two pancackes are allowed at luncheon (one egg each).

CREAMED HOT SOUP

    1 can asparagus
    1 can French-style string beans
    2 envelopes instant vegetable broth
  *2 teaspoons nonfat dry milk solids

Put all ingredients in blender including canned liquid. Blend ½ minute. Serve chilled or heat.

QUICK SOUP FOR ONE

  *6 ounces tomato juice
    1 envelope instant broth mix
    Cooked mushrooms or French-style string beans
      or both

Bring tomato juice to boil. Add other ingredients, heat and serve immediately.

VEGETABLE MINESTRONE SOUP

    1 small cabbage, shredded
    3 tablespoons dehydrated onion flakes
    2 stalks celery
    1 green pepper
    1 cup mushrooms
    1 cup green beans
    2 envelopes instant broth mix
    1½ cups water
  *1 cup tomato juice

Put everything into a kettle and cook until the vegetables are done.

VEGETABLE SOUP

    ½ cup cabbage, shredded
    1 cup celery with leaves, sliced
    Pepper
    Salt
    Paprika
    Onion flakes
  *1 cup tomato juice
    1 cup water

Simmer 1 hour on low flame.

Okay, so the baby's sick... your eating won't make him well!

Limited Vegetables

Select any one of the following vegetables and use at dinner only. Only one serving, or ½ cup, permitted. Vary your selections from day to day.

artichokes	oyster plant
bamboo shoots	parsnips
beets	peas
brussels sprouts	pumpkin
carrots	scallions
eggplant	squash (yellow)
green beans (mature)	tomato
okra	*tomato juice
onions	turnips

* Tomato juice may be taken at any time, limited to 12 ounces daily.

ARTICHOKE STUFFED WITH CRAB MEAT

*1 artichoke
*3 ounces canned shredded boned crab meat
¼ cup celery, cut fine
Tomato French Dressing W.W. (see index for
  recipe)

Wash each fresh artichoke under running cold water. Cut off the stem about 1 inch from the base. Cut off about 1 inch from the top, straight across. Rub with lemon juice to prevent blackening. Put into a large kettle of boiling salted water. Cover and cook about half an hour until the bottom is easily pierced with fork. Pour off water and turn each artichoke upside down. Remove choke with a spoon. Open petals out to form a cup. Combine crab meat, celery, and Tomato French Dressing W.W. to moisten. Fill artichoke with this mixture. Use one artichoke as limited vegetable.

ARTICHOKE HEARTS WITH HERBS

Cook *1 package (9 ounces) frozen artichoke hearts with 3 whole allspice, 1 small bay leaf, and ½ teaspoon salt, following label directions. Drain (save liquid for stews or health soup); remove allspice and bay leaf. Serves 2-3.

BAMBOO SHOOTS

One of the important foods in China and Japan, canned *bamboo shoots imported here may be added to salads, or served in a sauce made with 1 cup soy sauce, ¼ cup water and a dash of granulated sugar substitute. Simmer the sauce for 15 minutes before adding bamboo shoots.

* *Limited food—see Menu Plan, p. 18-20, for legal amount.*

WHITE DRAGON CABBAGE WITH BAMBOO SHOOTS

2 pounds cabbage (Chinese if possible)
*½ cup sliced bamboo shoots
3 medium dried Japanese mushrooms
1 teaspoon salt
¼ teaspoon MSG
Chicken stock or water

Wash the cabbage, remove tough stalk, cut it up and soak it in salted water. Soak mushrooms in water to cover. (Both should soak for about 15 minutes.) Drain mushrooms, saving the liquid; cut them in half. Add mushrooms to non-stick frying pan and stir-fry for a few minutes. Add cabbage and stir-fry for a minute more. Add bamboo shoots, salt, MSG, and ¼ cup of the mushroom liquid. If the cabbage seems to be dry, add another ¼ cup liquid (chicken stock if available, otherwise water). Cover and cook for about 10 minutes. Cabbage should be done but still crisp, not at all soggy.

QUICK COOKED BEETS

Peel tender *beets with a sharp knife, slice them thin or put them through a food chopper. Add very little water—about ¼ cup—and cook 15 minutes. Squeeze lemon juice, salt and pepper over them and a soupçon of sugar substitute. Serve at once.

BEET RELISH

*1 cup canned cook beets
¼ cup dehydrated onion flakes, covered with
vinegar
Granulated sugar substitute

Drain sliced, shredded or whole small beets, add onion flakes covered with vinegar, and sprinkle lightly with granulated sugar substitute. Chill and serve. Count ½ cup as serving of one limited vegetable.

QUICK BORSHT

Borsht is nourishing and economical, easily made and filling and there are as many different versions of borsht as there are spellings. This recipe uses beets but others use cabbage, beef bones, etc.

    4 bouillon cubes
    4 cups boiling water
  *½ cup raw grated beets
    2 tablespoons lemon juice or vinegar
    Salt and pepper to taste

Dissolve bouillon in boiling water, add beets, lemon juice, salt, and pepper and cook in covered pot for 15 minutes. Serve hot or chill and serve cold. Good as a summer soup with a spoonful of Sour Cream W.W. and slices of cucumber added to bowls just before serving.

BORSHT

  *6 large beets, peeled
    6 cups beef stock (if made from beef and bones,
        be sure to skim off any fat which rises to top
        after cooling)
    Salt
    Pepper
    1 tablespoon lemon juice or vinegar
    ¼ teaspoon granulated sugar substitute

Peel the beets; shred fine. Cover them with the stock and cook until beets are soft. Add salt, pepper and lemon juice or vinegar; cook 30 minutes more. Then stir in sugar substitute. Eat the borsht hot or cold. Six servings; count 1 limited vegetable for each serving.

Note: Borsht may also be made with mushroom stock to replace beef stock.

BORSHT WITH CABBAGE AND BEETS

1 cup celery, finely diced (include leaves and
    stalks)
*½ cup carrots (finely diced)
*½ cup onions, diced
  2 cups finely shredded cabbage
*1 cup tomato juice
  2 cups chicken stock (or 3 chicken broth powder
    packets and 2 cups water)
*1 cup shredded canned beets
  ½ teaspoon liquid sugar substitute
  Salt to taste

Cover celery, carrots, and onions with boiling water (about 1½ cups). Cook covered for 30 minutes. Add cabbage, tomato juice, chicken stock and beets. Cook 30-45 minutes more. Add sugar substitute and salt to taste. Stir and serve. Let soup cool uncovered (or with cover partly off). Cover and refrigerate. It will last for days. If soup gets too thick, stir in hot water and chicken stock. Four servings; each counts as 1 limited vegetable.

BRUSSELS SPROUTS

Soak these *tiny cabbages—that is what they are—in cold water for 10 minutes. Drain; cut a crosswise gash in stem end. Put into saucepan with 2 teaspoons caraway seed, ¼ teaspoon thyme, and salt. Cook until tender but still green (15-20 minutes). One-half cup counts as one limited vegetable.

BRUSSELS SPROUTS WITH CHEESE SAUCE

Grate *¾ ounce cheddar or American cheese and sprinkle it over freshly cooked *brussels sprouts. Serve immediately or put into low oven (250°F.) until cheese melts.

CARROTS

Cooked *carrots by themselves are quite dull. However, they take on personality when combined with cooked (unlimited) mushrooms and garnished with chopped parsley or chives.

To prepare young carrots scrub them with a brush and cook them in a skillet holding very little salted water. Cover and let steam until tender. Cooking time depends on size the carrot is cut. Young carrots cut in small dice take 8-10 minutes. A little bit of sugar substitute to bring out the sweetness of the vegetable may be added. One-half cup equals one limited vegetable.

HOW TO BUY CARROTS

Those tough old *carrots wrapped in cellophane bags (the stripes printed on the bag often have more good carrot color than the contents) are about as tasty and nutritive as an old rubber ball. Carrots which are fresh should come in bunches with their tops on. Try to find a store which sells them freshly dug and unpackaged.

CARROT JUICE

The water in which you cooked the carrots is good to drink. Season to taste with salt, pepper, finely chopped parsley and dill too.

CARROT MILK

Put *1 cup skim milk in blender with *2 medium carrots, cut into pieces. Blend until completely liquefied. Serve cold or heat gently and quickly to preserve good carrot flavor. Young Weight Watchers enjoy this for its pretty tint and good taste. Two servings.

CARROT RING

Put freshly cooked *carrots through a ricer or mash with potato masher. Add 1 tablespoon chopped chives. Put into small ring mold. A dash of sugar substitute may be added. Heat in 350°F. oven or on top of stove in pan holding a little water. Invert mold and fill center with French-style green beans. Surround with whole raw mushroom caps dipped in lemon juice and alternate with bunches of parsley.

CARROT SOUP

Combine ¾ cup water, beef bouillon cube, and *¼ cup diced tender carrot (scrubbed clean). Put into blender and blend for 1 minute. Heat gently without boiling and serve hot.

SKILLET CARROTS AND GREEN BEANS

Nice change: Cut *carrots in long strips, cover with boiling water and cook in skillet for 5 minutes. Season with salt and pepper. Add package of frozen French-style green beans and cook 8 minutes longer until done. There should be no more than ½ cup water in the pan when you add the beans. Chopped fresh fine herbs added for the last few minutes make this a treat. Parsley and chives are good additions.

BAKED EGGPLANT SLICES

Cut an unpeeled washed *eggplant into slices about ½-inch thick. Marinate in Tomato French Dressing W.W. for 15 minutes. Bake in 400°F. oven, until eggplant is done, 10 to 12 minutes. Turn slices once. Surround with parsley sprigs. (Cut clove of garlic may be brushed over eggplant before it is marinated.)

BROILED EGGPLANT

Prepare *eggplant as for Baked Eggplant but put under broiler; turn once to broil both sides. If eggplant is dry baste with Dill Marinade. 3-4 slices make 1 serving.

EGGPLANT CASSEROLE

*1 medium eggplant cut in ½-inch cubes
*1 cup Tomato Sauce (see index for recipe)
½ cup water
*1 medium onion, diced
1 small green pepper, diced
1 stalk celery, diced
1 small can mushrooms
Garlic powder, salt, oregano

Parboil eggplant for 6 minutes, drain and place in bowl. Combine other ingredients. Arrange in layers in casserole alternating with eggplant. Bake 1 hour in 350°F. oven. Four servings.

HERBED EGGPLANT

Cube an unpeeled *eggplant and brown without fat in heated heavy pan. Season with salt and pepper. Cover with chicken stock (or instant chicken-broth mix and water), and cook until eggplant is soft —20 minutes or so. Add 1 tablespoon basil or other fresh herb and 1 tablespoon chopped parsley. Heat long enough to extract flavor from herbs.

EGGPLANT HORS D'OEUVRE

Cover washed *eggplant with boiling water and cook until soft, 15 to 20 minutes. Let cool. Discard top of stem. Remove skin. Chop pulp. Season with salt, freshly ground pepper and a dash of lemon juice. Onion flakes or onion juice may also be added. Surround with parsley sprigs. Serve as an hors d'oeuvre with cucumber slices for dipping. Count ½ cup as 1 limited vegetable.

PARTY EGGPLANT

Cut small *eggplants into halves. Scoop out pulp, leaving a strong shell. Put shell into cold salted water until ready to fill. Boil the pulp in salted water to cover, adding the pulp of another peeled diced *eggplant. Combine with sliced raw mushrooms over which you have sprinkled lemon juice. Season with salt and pepper, and fill eggplant shell. Refrigerate, covered with wax paper, until ready to bake, then put into shallow pan in 425°F. oven until brown. Garnish with strips of pimento and serve hot or cold. Limited vegetable.

SPANISH EGGPLANT

   *1 unpeeled egglant, cubed
   1 green pepper, cut into squares
   1 stalk celery, sliced
   *Tomato juice
   Salt
   Freshly ground pepper
   Onion flakes

Brown eggplant, green pepper and celery in heated heavy pan without adding fat. Turn frequently to prevent scorching. When brown, cover with tomato juice and season with salt, pepper and lots of onion flakes. Let cook, covered, at least 40 minutes. ¾ cup makes 1 serving. Serve hot or cold. Excellent supper dish with allotted frankfurters, cooked first to remove fat, then sliced and heated on top of stove.

TURKISH EGGPLANT CAVIAR

Bake whole *eggplant in 375°F. oven until soft or put on rack over gas flame and let cook slowly until done, turning to bake all sides. As soon as cool enough to handle, remove skin and let drain well. Chop cooled eggplant with *1 small diced onion and ¼ cup diced celery. Season to taste with salt and freshly ground pepper. Fresh minced herbs—parsley, basil or dill—are a nice addition. (The eggplant, onion and celery may also be put into blender). Count ½ cup as 1 limited vegetable.

FENNEL

Known as finocchio, anise, or Italian fennel, this unusual vegetable may be bought in most Italian neighborhoods and is easy to grow in your vegetable garden. Serve it raw—allowing 1 small bulb for each serving—or cut the stem into pieces and cook until tender in a small amount of boiling salted water. It makes a pleasant surprise for the taste buds; how often do they find a vegetable which looks like celery and tastes like licorice?

* *Limited food—see Menu Plan, p. 18-20, for legal amount.*

OKRA

*Okra has a very individual flavor and you either like it enormously or can't be bothered with it. Steam it in a small amount of boiling salted water (about ⅛ inch at bottom of pan) and serve it hot or cold as salad. Limited vegetable.

OKRA SOUP (CHICKEN GUMBO)

   *1½ cup canned sliced okra
   *½ cup chopped onion
    ¼ cup chopped green pepper
    1 quart chicken broth (fat-free chicken soup or
       packets of powdered mix diluted with water)
   *2½ cups tomato juice
    Small bay leaf
    1 tablespoon chopped parsley
    Salt and pepper to taste

Brown okra, onion, and green pepper in heavy dry hot saucepan until soft. Stir to prevent scorching. Add chicken broth, tomato juice, and bay leaf. Simmer for 15 minutes. Add parsley and salt and pepper. Okra and onion are limited vegetables; if this soup is divided into 8 portions, count each one as ¼ limited vegetable; 5 ounces tomato juice.

BROWNING ONIONS

*Onions brown faster when started in a hot dry skillet without fat. Peel onions first, of course, then cut in slices. Brown them in hot skillet, stirring so that they do not scorch. Add chicken stock, about ¼ cup at a time, and cover pan to cook onions till soft.

SMOTHERED ONIONS

Peel and slice *3 onions, brown in hot dry skillet, then cover and cook until soft, adding a little water if necessary. Season with a dash of Worcestershire sauce and salt and pepper. Serve with meat, fish or vegetables. Three servings, each counting as 1 limited vegetable.

FRENCH ONION SOUP

Peel and slice *3 onions and brown in hot dry skillet. Add 4 cups stock (may be made with mix for instant chicken or beef broth). Cover and simmer for ½ hour. Season with salt and pepper, ½ teaspoon Worcestershire sauce and a dash of artificial butter flavor. Pour into large casserole or into 4 individual casseroles and put into hot oven, 450°F., for about 10 minutes or brown under broiler. Serve hot. Makes 3 servings, each counting as 1 limited vegetable.

BLENDER ONION SOUP

Add *2 cups skim milk and 2 tablespoons finely chopped parsley to French Onion Soup. However, instead of transferring to casserole, put into blender and whirl until parsley is finely cut.

OYSTER VEGETABLE PLANT OR SALSIFY

If you should happen to find *this parsnipy plant at an Italian greengrocer's, take it home, remove its brown covering, rub it with a cut lemon (to prevent discoloration) and cook, covered, in 1 inch of boiling salted water for about 10 minutes. When tender, slice and serve as salad sprinkled with one of the salad dressings and garnished with water cress. Buon gusto! (A limited vegetable.)

PARSNIPS

Scrape *parsnips and parboil them in boiling salted water for 10 minutes. Cut in half lengthwise and bake in shallow baking pan. Sprinkle with granulated sugar substitute and artificial butter flavor before serving.

GREEN PEAS

Buy full-podded *peas with good dark green color. Cook uncovered in just enough boiling salted water to keep them from scorching. Allow about 10 minutes. Season with salt and pepper (and if you like, add some artificial butter flavor). Serve hot. One pound of peas in the pod, after shelling, will make about 1 cup. Serves 2. While peas are cooking, mushrooms (unlimited) may be browned in hot dry skillet with a couple of tablespoons of chicken stock, then added to cooked peas.

PEAS FRANCAISE

> ½ head lettuce, cut into wedges
> *2 cups fresh peas
> ¼ cup water
> Onion juice or onion flakes
> Salt
> Pepper
> Drop of liquid sugar substitute

Put lettuce, peas, water and onion into casserole. Season with salt, pepper and sugar substitute. Cover tightly and bake for 45 minutes while you are baking chicken or apples. Serve ½ cup peas as 1 limited vegetable.

* *Limited food—see Menu Plan, p. 18-20, for legal amount.*

SPLIT PEA SOUP

>   *½ cup canned peas
> ½ cup chicken stock
> Dash of onion juice (scrape cut onion with a
>   knife
> Dash of curry powder

Combine ingredients in blender and purée for a few seconds; heat without boiling) and serve hot. Delicious. (Lacking a blender, you can mash peas or put through food mill). One serving; one limited vegetable.

HOW TO COOK PUMPKIN

Wash *pumpkin and cut in half crosswise. Remove strings and seeds. Bake in baking pan, shell side up in 350°F. oven, until tender. Scrape pulp from shell and serve mashed; ½ cup is 1 serving.

PUMPKIN SOUP

Put into blender (or use other food mill) *1 cup cooked pumpkin, 3 cups chicken broth, ½ teaspoon salt, onion and celery salt, dash white pepper and the merest pinch of sugar substitute. Add *¼ cup skim milk, heat gently and bring to table.

WINTER SQUASH

Learn to recognize and use the different types of squash which are available all year. Winter squash is a limited vegetable; summer squash is unlimited.

Hubbard Squash. The most available winter type. Rough, warty, round, usually dark bronze-green or bluish grey, tough and hard.

To Prepare Hubbard Squash. Cut in half or leave whole and bake in pan in moderate to hot oven (350° to 425°F.) until soft. Serve in shell or remove and mash pulp. Mashed pulp may be seasoned with cinnamon, lemon juice and freshly ground black pepper.

Banana Squash. Shaped like a banana, and olive grey changing to creamy pink. This is a good variety for baking, with a sweet flavor. Cut in serving pieces and bake, cut side down, in shallow casserole holding a small amount of hot water, about 30 minutes at 375°F.

Butternut Squash. Shaped something like a pear. Skin should be pale creamy brown or dark yellow. Cut in half and steam in colander in small amount of water, or bake whole or in halves wrapped in aluminum foil. Serve with a dash of nutmeg and artificial sweetener if desired. Baking time will vary—usually 45 minutes to 1 hour.

Acorn Squash. Looks like acorn with dark green rind. Bake whole or cut in halves or in rings. Prepare like Butternut Squash.

ACORN SQUASH

Cut round green *squash in half and scoop out seeds. Preheat oven. Sprinkle drop of cinnamon and granulated sugar substitute and bake at 400°F. for ½ to ¾ hour. (Tastes like sweet potato. This is a limited vegetable—watch weight! To be used as a dinner vegetable.)

MOCK SWEET-POTATO PUDDING

     *1 package frozen squash
      ¼ teaspoon salt
      Dash of pepper
      1 teaspoon liquid sugar substitute
      ½ tablespoon grated orange rind or orange juice

Place squash, salt, pepper, sugar substitute and orange rind or juice in baking dish. Sprinkle top with cinnamon and bake uncovered in 350°F. oven for ½ hour.

BAKED TOMATOES

When the oven is on for fish, bake a *tomato and serve as (limited) vegetable. Cut an unpeeled tomato in half. Sprinkle with salt, pepper and a bit of grated onion. Bake about 20 minutes. Serve when tomato slices are brown. One tomato equals 1 limited vegetable.

TOMATO CASES

*Tomatoes used as shells or cases must be firm and of a good color. To prepare them as shells, peel them first (immerse them in boiling water or put fork into stem end and hold briefly over flame). Scoop out pulp from the center. Sprinkle inside with salt, invert on rack placed over plate and refrigerate. Fill with *tuna, *shrimp, or any *seafood salad. Good company meal in summer.

FRIED TOMATOES

Heat a small iron skillet. Meanwhile cut a *tomato in thick slices, sprinkle with a bit of liquid sugar substitute, salt, pepper, and some onion juice. Fry in hot skillet. Turn slices carefully so they don't break and brown other side.

STUFFED TOMATOES

Prepare *1 tomato for each serving as follows: Wash, dry and cut out stem with a small grapefruit knife to make a funnel shape. With a small spoon scoop out the tomato seeds (set them aside) and set the tomatoes upside down to drain. Cook the tomato seeds, juice drained from tomatoes, slices of mushrooms and onion seasoning, just long enough to soften mushrooms. Season to taste with salt and pepper and add herbs to taste: dill or parsley. Use to fill tomatoes. Garnish tops of tomatoes with bean sprouts marinated in Cucumber-Lemon Sauce (see index for recipe) and serve.

TOMATO BOUILLON

    1 can (10½ ounces) beef bouillon
    1 can (10½ ounces) cold water
  *1 #2 can tomato juice
    2 teaspoons dehydrated onion flakes
    3 stalks celery cut into 2-inch pieces
    Salt
    Red pepper

Combine in saucepan bouillon, water, tomato juice, onion, and celery. Simmer 20 minutes, strain. Season to taste with salt and red pepper. Serve in soup bowls; add a slice of lemon which has been dipped in parsley in each bowl. 6 servings. *Croutons made from toasting bread from day's allowance may be used at luncheon.

TOMATO BOUILLON ON THE ROCKS

    ¼ cup diced celery
  *¼ cup diced carrots
  *¼ cup chopped onion
    2 sprigs parsley
  *4 cups tomato juice
    ⅛ to ¼ teaspoon white pepper
    6 whole cloves
    1 bay leaf
    1 teaspoon salt
    ⅛ teaspoon dried thyme
    2 cups canned beef bouillon or consommé, chilled
    6 lemon slices
    6 green *scallions or celery sticks

In large saucepan, combine all ingredients except bouillon, lemon slices, and scallions or celery sticks. Bring to boil; cover; simmer over low heat 1 hour. Strain; then refrigerate. *15 minutes before serving:*

Combine chilled tomato mixture with bouillon. Serve in Old-Fashioned glasses, one-fourth filled with crushed ice. Garnish each with a lemon slice which has been snipped in center and has a scallion threaded through this center. Makes 6 servings.

great for "Cocktail Time"!

Serve in Old-Fashioned glass.

Lemon slice placed in center cut.

Remember...

you don't need alcohol to get your "kicks"... you'll get them from a size 9 dress.

BLOODY MARY

*1 cup tomato juice
Dash Worcestershire sauce
Dash lemon juice
Salt
Pepper
¼ teaspoon white horseradish

Mix all ingredients in tall glass. Pour over ice.

CUCUMBER AND TOMATO COCKTAIL

  *¾ cup tomato juice
  1 teaspoon lemon juice
  6 thin slices cucumber
  ½ cup finely cracked ice

Put into blender and whiz until smooth, about half a minute. Season to taste with salt and dill, or any other desired seasoning. Serve immediately. 1 serving. (You can crack ice cubes by wrapping them in towel, then pounding with a mallet, hammer, rolling pin, etc.)

HEALTH COCKTAIL

  *2 cups tomato juice
  1 small stalk celery, with leaves, diced
  ¼ cup parsley sprigs
  2 slices lemon with peel
  1 slice onion
  ¼ teaspoon salt
  Dash of granulated sugar substitute (optional)

Put into blender and run at high speed until all vegetables are liquefied. Serves 4.

SOBER OX ON THE ROCKS

Beef broth over ice, with a dash of Worcestershire sauce. Sprinkle with celery salt and serve with a lemon slice or wedge.

  * *Limited food—you are allowed 12 ounces daily.*

HOT TOMATO PUNCH

Lemon gives a nice lift to the beef broth.

> *1 46-ounce can (about 6 cups) tomato juice
> 1 can condensed beef broth
> 1 teaspoon horseradish
> 2 teaspoons Worcestershire sauce
> ½ teaspoon onion salt
> Few drops Tabasco sauce
> 1 lemon, sliced thin
> Whole cloves

In saucepan, combine juice, beef broth, horseradish, Worcestershire, onion salt, and Tabasco. Cut lemon slices in thirds; stud with cloves; add to juice and heat just to boiling. Serve immediately, a lemon-slice floater in each cup. Makes 8 to 10 servings.

TOMATO-SAUERKRAUT COCKTAIL

For the pause that refreshes, equal amount of sauerkraut juice and *tomato juice, with salt, pepper, served with cracked ice make a good cocktail. Count only the tomato juice—sauerkraut juice is unlimited.

TOMATO SOUP

> *8 ounces tomato juice
> 1 bouillon cube
> Dash garlic powder
> Salt
> Pepper
> Mushroom Purée (see index for recipe), sautéed
>   mushrooms, or mushroom liquid to taste

Heat tomato juice, add bouillon cube dissolved in 6 ounces water, garlic, salt and pepper to taste. Also if desired add mushrooms. Makes a delicious soup.

THICK TOMATO SOUP

A cup of *tomato juice put into the blender with a slice of *bread from luncheon allowance, cut up, equals a thick tomato soup. Serve hot or cold.

JELLIED TOMATO SALAD

   1 package plain gelatin
 *1½ cups tomato juice
   1 tablespoon horseradish
   1 tablespoon lemon juice or vinegar
   1 cup celery (or shredded cabbage) sliced thin
   1 tablespoon minced onion
   2 tablespoons chopped pickle relish
   Salt and pepper to taste

Sprinkle gelatin over tomato juice in saucepan, then heat slowly until gelatin is dissolved. Add horseradish, and lemon juice or vinegar; cool until gelatin thickens. Stir in celery (or cabbage), onion, pickle relish and salt and pepper to taste. Chill in ring mold. Unmold on large platter. Heap center with *cottage cheese sprinkled with chopped chives, surround with water cress, and serve for luncheon. Another good combination: marinate cooked cold vegetables in Creole Sauce and use to fill center of ring. Four to six servings.

Unflavored gelatin is unlimited.

VEGETABLE TOMATO ASPIC

    1 tablespoon unflavored gelatin
  *1¾ cups tomato juice
    2 tablespoons lemon juice
    2 tablespoons grated onion
    ¼ teaspoon salt
    ½ teaspoon Worcestershire sauce
    ⅛ teaspoon Tabasco sauce
    1 cup shredded cabbage
    ½ cup chopped celery
  *½ cup grated carrots
    ½ cup chopped green pepper

Sprinkle gelatin over ½ cup cold tomato juice. Add 1¼ cups of tomato juice. Add lemon juice, onion, salt, Worcestershire sauce, and Tabasco sauce. Chill. When mixture has consistency of thin syrup, fold in cabbage, celery, carrots, and green pepper. Chill in mold. Unmold. Garnish with parsley sprigs or salad greens.

OLD VIRGINIA TOMATO ASPIC

  *3 cups tomato juice
    ½ cup chicken stock
    2 stalks celery
    1 sprig parsley
    Dash of sugar substitute
    1 teaspoon salt
    Dash cayenne
    2 teaspoons dehydrated onion flakes
    2 tablespoons gelatin
    ½ cup cold water
    1½ tablespoons lemon juice

Simmer together first eight ingredients. Strain. Soak gelatin in water and lemon juice and dissolve in hot strained mixture. Pour into wet mold. Chill. Fill with *crab meat or *tuna salad.

GARDEN-FLOWER SALAD

Cut a *tomato into sections, but don't cut all the way down—be sure to leave a base. Flatten the sections a bit so they look like flower petals. In the center pile flowerets of cooked broccoli. Between the petals place flowerets of cooked cauliflower. Serve with Pimento French Dressing W.W.

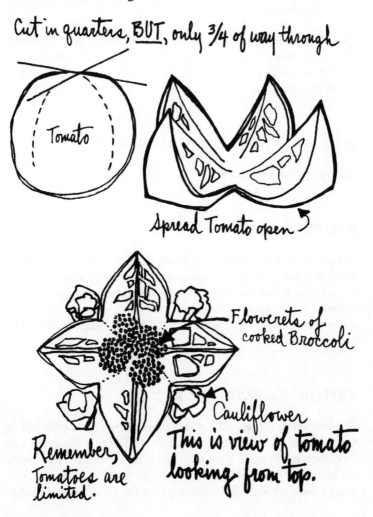

Cut in quarters, BUT, only ¾ of way through

Tomato

spread Tomato open

Flowerets of cooked Broccoli

Cauliflower

Remember, Tomatoes are limited.

This is view of tomato looking from top.

JELLIED MADRILENE

A summer delight.

    2 envelopes plain gelatin
    *3½ cups tomato juice
    Lemon wedges
    Cucumber slices

Sprinkle gelatin over ½ cup tomato juice. Dissolve over low heat. Add 1 cup tomato juice and heat. Add 2 cups cold tomato juice. Refrigerate until set. Spoon into individual bowls, serve with a wedge of lemon and slices of cucumber. 8 servings.

WEIGHT WATCHERS "SANDWICH"

Slices of *tomatoes filled with *fish salad.

WHITE TURNIPS

Parboil small young *turnips without peeling them. Boil in salted water to cover with 1 teaspoon caraway seeds and a sprinkling of onion flakes. When tender, peel turnips and serve as is or thoroughly mashed. A half teaspoon of dried basil or 1 teaspoon freshly cut leaves may be added for good flavor. One-half cup equals 1 limited vegetable.

YELLOW TURNIPS OR RUTABAGAS

Quarter *turnips, peel and cut into cubes. Cover them with boiling water and cook until soft (30 minutes). Drain well, mash with fork, then put through strainer or purée in a blender. Heat (without boiling) *¼ cup skim milk in saucepan, add mashed or puréed turnips and cook and stir until turnips are the consistency of mashed potatoes. (You may whip turnips as they cook.) Season with salt, pepper and paprika and serve.

Nice variation: Mound turnips on aluminum foil and brown under broiler when broiling fish.

RUTABAGAS

Quarter *turnips, peel and cut into large dice. Cook covered until they are barely soft (10 minutes). Place in casserole. For each half cup, combine ¼ cup low-calorie lemon soda, 2 packets granulated sugar substitute and cinnamon. Add to turnips in casserole. Cover and bake until turnips are tender.

Spring cleaning time !

Get rid of those foods that "clutter-up" your figure !!!

BAKED RUTABAGA

Bake the yellow *turnip without peeling it for about 40 minutes or until tender. Cut it open and garnish with minced parsley and a few raw chopped spinach leaves. A sprinkling of lemon juice adds a refreshing tang.

GAZPACHO (Cold Spanish Soup)

    ½ green pepper, in 1-inch pieces
   *1 cup onions, cut up
    ½ cucumber, unpeeled, in 1-inch slices
    1 stalk celery, in 1-inch slices
    Water
    1 beef-bouillon cube
    1 cup hot water
    ½ peeled clove garlic
   *2 ripe tomatoes, quartered
    Dash Tabasco sauce
    1 sprig parsley
    1 teaspoon salt
    ¼ cup favorite salad dressing (see index)
   *2 cups canned tomato juice

Place first four ingredients in electric-blender container with water to cover. Cover and blend at low speed for 3 seconds. Transfer from blender container to large bowl. Soften bouillon in hot water a few minutes. Place in electric-blender container with all remaining ingredients. Cover and blend at high speed about 1 minute. Pour over drained vegetables in bowl and stir. Refrigerate, covered, for at least 4 hours, preferably overnight. Serves 8, one-half limited vegetable per serving. If desired, float ice cube in each serving.

* *Limited food—see Menu Plan, p. 18-20, for legal amount.*

JELLIED GAZPACHO

> 1 envelope plain gelatin
> 1½ cups water
> 1 bouillon cube
> ⅓ cup vinegar or lemon juice
> 1 teaspoon salt
> 1 teaspoon paprika
> ½ teaspoon basil
> ¼ teaspoon ground cloves
> ⅛ teaspoon Tabasco sauce
> 1 clove garlic, minced
> *2 tablespoons finely chopped onion
> ¼ cup finely chopped green pepper
> *1½ cups finely chopped fresh tomatoes

Soften gelatin by sprinkling it over ½ cup water. Place over low heat and stir until gelatin is dissolved. Remove from heat. Add bouillon cube, stir until dissolved. Add remaining 1 cup water, vinegar or lemon juice, salt, paprika, basil, cloves, and Tabasco. Mix well. Chill in refrigerator until gelatin has consistency of thin syrup. Fold in garlic, onion, celery, green pepper and tomatoes. Cover and chill about 2 hours. Serve in soup bowls for a refreshing summer soup. Serves 8. Count each serving as one-half limited vegetable.

SUMMER DINNER

Jellied Gazpacho
Fillet of Flounder Marguerite, p. 67
Cole Slaw, p. 153
   Tossed with ¼ cup fresh green beans
Baked Apple

VEGETABLE MINESTRONE

Note: If using canned or frozen vegetables, add them in last ¾ hour of cooking.

    *1 cup diced carrots
    *1 cup diced turnips
     1 cup young green beans, cut French-style
     1 small cabbage, soaked 10 minutes in salt water,
        cut into 8 wedges and sliced
     ½ cup sliced green squash
    *½ cup minced onions or leeks
     ½ cup diced celery
     ½ cup cut-up spinach leaves (discard tough stems)
     ½ cup fresh parsley
     1 clove garlic
     1 tablespoon salt
    *1½ cups fresh or canned tomatoes, chopped
     1 teaspoon minced basil
     Pepper to taste
     2 quarts soup stock or consommé without fat (or
        8 bouillion cubes dissolved in 2 quarts hot
        water—a large soup bone can be added too)

Combine all ingredients in a large soup kettle and bring to boil, then cover and cook gently for 1½ hours. Serve in large soup bowls. 8 servings; count each as one-half limited vegetable.
    Try with bean sprouts too.

QUICK VEGETABLE SOUP

    *½ cup chopped onion
     ½ cup cabbage, shredded
     1 cup celery with leaves
    *½ cup diced carrots
     6 peppercorns

*2 cups tomato juice
4 cups water
1 envelope instant chicken broth mix
Paprika
1 teaspoon salt

Combine and let simmer for ¾ to 1 hour on low flame. Serves 4;
each serving counts as ½ limited vegetable.

GREEK VEGETABLE STEW

*2 chopped onions
6 zucchini, cut up
1 pound green string beans, broken in half
*1 cup yellow squash, sliced
1 to 2 cups celery leaves
1 package frozen or fresh chopped spinach
*4 tomatoes, quartered
1 teaspoon salt
4 cups water
8 slices lemon

Lightly brown onions in a hot dry skillet. Add remaining ingredients. Cook covered 40 minutes, stirring occasionally. Serve with a
lemon slice in each bowl. 8 servings; each serving equals 1 limited
vegetable.

RATATOUILLE

*2 pounds eggplant
2 pounds zucchini
1 pound green pepper
*2 cups tomato juice
2 cloves garlic
Salt and pepper

Wash but do not peel vegetables. Cut them into even dice. Brown in heavy heated pan, turning to prevent scorching. Add other ingredients, cover and cook at least ¾ hour until eggplant is done. Add tomato juice as needed. Eat hot or cold, or reheat if desired. Green beans, cauliflower and onion flakes are all good additions. Makes about 4 servings.

SAVORY TOMATOES, SQUASH AND GREEN BEANS

    *1 large diced onion
    1 clove garlic
    ½ cup minced parsley
    ½ cup chicken consommé
    2 teaspoons salt
    ¼ teaspoon pepper
    ¼ teaspoon thyme
    ¼ teaspoon sage
    1 pound French-style green beans
    *3 diced tomatoes
    *2 cups diced yellow squash
    2 cups water or consommé

Cook onion, garlic and parsley in ½ cup chicken consommé. When onions are soft add remaining ingredients, cover and cook until green beans are soft. 8 servings; 1 limited vegetable each.

CASSEROLE OF VEGETABLES

    ¾ pound green beans, cut French style
    *1 cup small white onions
    ½ pound mushrooms
    ½ cup chicken stock

*¼ cup nonfat dry milk solids
4 green peppers
*1 cup tomatoes
Salt and pepper to taste
Worcestershire sauce

About an hour before serving, cook beans in boiling salted water for 10 minutes, until they are barely tender. Drain and set aside. Peel onions. Cook until barely tender. Drain and set aside. Slice mushrooms and cook in chicken stock until tender, about 3 minutes. Stir in milk solids. Set aside. Cut peppers in half lengthwise and take out seeds. Arrange pepper shells in a cross in the middle of a large round shallow casserole. Between each section put white onions. Put the green beans in a circle as a border. Put mushrooms into green peppers. Combine tomatoes, salt, pepper and Worcestershire sauce. Stir well. Divide them equally over the vegetables in casserole. Bake at 375-425°F. for about half an hour. Serve from casserole. Four servings. Count each serving as 1 limited vegetable.

MIXED VEGETABLE SALAD

1 cup cooked, cut-up asparagus
*1 cup diced beets, drained
1 cup celery slices
1 cup cooked green beans
½ cup green pepper
1 teaspoon onion juice
Salt
Paprika
Tomato French Dressing (see index for recipe)

Combine vegetables, add seasonings, and cover with Tomato French Dressing. Serve in bowls with celery or spinach leaves as garnish. Four servings; count each as ½ limited vegetable.

VEGETABLE GHIVETCH

This is popular with Romanians, and you will enjoy it too, for it is colorful and makes an interesting medley of flavors. Use fresh vegetables only.

> 1 red pepper, sliced across
> 1 cup young green beans, sliced lengthwise
> 1 small head cabbage, cut into thick pieces
> 1 small head cauliflower, cut into thick pieces
> 1 summer squash, sliced lengthwise
> 1 cup spinach leaves, hard rib removed
> 1 cup mushrooms, sliced lengthwise
> 6 short stalks asparagus
> 1 bunch herbs—parsley, dill (whatever is available)
> 4 pieces garlic, slightly mashed
> ½ cup dehydrated onion flakes
> 2 cups boiling soup stock
> 2 teaspoons salt
> Freshly grated pepper

Use a very large shallow casserole and lightly mix vegetables in it. Sprinkle with herbs. Spear the garlic with toothpicks so that you can find and remove the pieces before serving. Add to casserole. Bring onion flakes and soup stock to a boil, and pour over vegetables in casserole. Season to taste with salt and pepper. Cover and bake in a moderate oven until liquid is absorbed and vegetables are soft. Serve hot or cold. All the vegetables in this recipe are unlimited, but ghivetch is often made with sliced carrots, cubed turnips, green peas, cubed parsley roots, chopped leeks, okra, and unpeeled eggplant pieces (all limited vegetables) in addition.

* Limited food—see Menu Plan, p. 18-20, for legal amount.

Dressings and Sauces

The sauces, dressings, and dips in this chapter may be used at any time and in any amount, except for those containing ingredients which are marked with an asterisk. Ingredients marked with an asterisk are limited, must be totaled in your daily count, and must not exceed your daily allowance.

You will find it helpful to make up a small quantity of several different dressings and sauces. Store each kind in a small jar in the refrigerator, using a strip of freezer tape as a label. The following sauces and dressings are recommended for your basic inventory, but do try some of the others too, and make changes in your basic stock from time to time.

> Blender Basil Dressing
> Chambord Sauce
> Chinese Sweet and Sour Sauce
> Creole Sauce
> Tomato French Dressing

BBQ BASTE

> *½ cup tomato juice
> ½ teaspoon salt
> ½ teaspoon dry mustard
> ½ teaspoon sugar substitute
> Dash of chili powder
> Dash of pepper
> 1 cup water

Mix tomato juice, salt, mustard, sugar substitute, chili powder and pepper in small bowl; gradually stir in water. Use as baste for meat or chicken.

COOKED BARBECUE SAUCE

> *1 cup tomato juice
> 1 envelope powdered mix for chicken broth
> 3 tablespoons lemon juice or vinegar
> 2 tablespoons Worcestershire sauce
> 1 clove garlic
> ¾ teaspoon dry mustard
> 1 teaspoon dehydrated onion flakes
> ½ teaspoon paprika
> Dash coarse black pepper
> ½ envelope granulated sugar substitute
> Cayenne pepper, or hot red tepini pepper (the
>   kind that comes with pickling spice)

Heat in saucepan until thickened. Use as baste over chicken, chops, hamburgers, frankfurters, etc.

BECHAMEL SAUCE FOR FISH

Thicken fish stock (see index) by adding *bread crumbs made from daily bread (slightly stale bread is best) puréed in blender. Heat and serve over cooked *fish for luncheon.

BLENDER BASIL DRESSING

> 4 tablespoons wine vinegar
> 2 tablespoons water
> ¼ teaspoon salt
> ¼ teaspoon sugar substitute
> ½ teaspoon basil leaves
> 1 clove garlic
> 1 tablespoon chives

Put all ingredients in blender for 2 minutes. Good over lamb or as dressing for greens.

BLENDER SAUCE LOUISIANA STYLE

> 1 tablespoon dehydrated onion flakes
> ½ green pepper, sliced
> Chicken stock or beef bouillon (may be made
>   with instant mix)
> *1 cup tomato juice
> 1 clove garlic (optional)
> 1 teaspoon salt
> Freshly ground black pepper
> ¼ teaspoon sugar substitute
> Dash of Tabasco sauce

Cook onion flakes and green pepper in chicken stock or beef bouillon to cover for 5 minutes. Put into blender container with remaining ingredients and liquefy. Serve hot with fish fillets.

CELERY SAUCE

> 9-10 stalks celery (including green tops)
> 2 teaspoons instant onion (optional)
> Water to cover
> 1 envelope instant chicken broth mix

Cut the celery into a large saucepan, add onion flakes if you are using them, and water to cover. Cook rapidly uncovered until celery is soft and water is reduced to little more than a cup. If the water evaporates too quickly, add more to be sure that the celery is cooked through. After about an hour of cooking the sauce, stir in chicken-broth mix; after a minute, turn off heat and purée the vegetable and liquid in a blender. Lacking a blender, you can use a food mill or the fine blade of a food chopper. Season with salt and pepper and use as a sauce over fish, vegetables, eggs, etc. There is no limit on the quantity that Weight Watchers may use; therefore, I recommend that you make up a quantity of this good sauce and find room to store it in your refrigerator.

Note: Additional seasonings which may be puréed with vegetables include dill leaves, lemon slice, chives, and parsley.

CHEESE SAUCE (Limited)

Cut up *1 ounce hard cheese. Heat with *skim milk and add paprika. Serve it over any cooked unlimited vegetable as a luncheon dish. It is excellent over cooked asparagus, cauliflower, young green beans, etc. To complete the luncheon, it may be served with a half portion (2 ounces) of tuna, chicken or other allowed luncheon food, or over 1 sliced hard-cooked egg.

CHAMBORD SAUCE

> 3 tablespoons prepared mustard (a Dijon type is
>   good)
> *1 cup skim milk
> 1 clove whole garlic, peeled
> Salt and pepper to taste
> 1½ tablespoons lemon juice
> 2 teaspoons instant beef broth mix (undiluted
>   powder)

Heat mustard over a very low flame in a heavy skillet and stir in milk. Add garlic, salt, pepper, lemon and beef broth concentrate. Simmer slowly about 10 minutes but do not let it boil. Remove garlic and serve sauce in a heated sauce bowl. Good over broiled veal chops or any bland meat or fish. One delicious addition is *2 tablespoons Sour Cream W.W. slowly heated; another is diced pimentos.

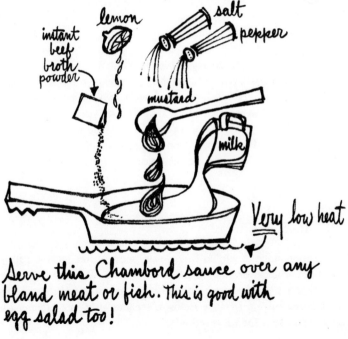

Serve this Chambord sauce over any bland meat or fish. This is good with egg salad too!

CHEESE-TOMATO SAUCE

Follow recipe for Cheese Sauce but substitute *tomato juice for skim milk, and season with salt, cayenne pepper and a sprinkle of onion juice (cut an onion and extract some juice with a spoon or knife). Deduct cheese from daily allowance.

CHIFFON SALAD DRESSING

*½ cup tomato juice
Juice of half lemon
Garlic powder
1 teaspoon grated onion or onion flakes
1 teaspoon rosemary, fresh if possible, or
   ½ teaspoon dried
Salt
Pepper
*Yolk of hard-boiled egg

Put everything but egg yolk into blender container and turn blender on for about 15 seconds. Add mashed yolk of egg and serve. Make a refreshing summer luncheon salad with two varieties of lettuce, young spinach leaves, cucumbers, radishes, red peppers, and slices of hard-cooked egg. The salad materials should be well washed, well dried, and crisped in the refrigerator before serving. The egg white left from this dressing can be cut up and sprinkled over the salad.

CORAL SAUCE

Add lemon juice to Onion Sauce, salt, pepper and lots of paprika and heat. Pour over canned drained *salmon. Broil or bake until salmon is hot. A good sauce for asparagus, cabbage or broccoli. Heat sauce before using. If sauce seems to separate, put into blender container and blend for a few seconds.

PINK CRANBERRY CREAM DRESSING

   *½ heaping cup fresh cranberries (counts as 1 fruit)
   ¾ tablespoon liquid sugar substitute
   2 tablespoons water
   ¼ teaspoon salt
   1 tablespoon lemon juice
   *½ cup Whipped Topping W.W. # 1 (see index
      for recipe)

Put into blender container the cranberries, sugar substitute, water
and salt. Blend for 15-20 seconds. Cool, add lemon juice. Fold in
Whipped Topping. Serve over orange or grapefruit sections, cut-up
pineapple, or other allowed fruit. Or serve it over cooked rhubarb
which is unlimited.

CREOLE SAUCE

   1 green pepper, diced
   2 tablespoons diced celery
   3 tablespoons juice scraped from cut onion or
      dehydrated onion flakes
   1 envelope instant chicken broth
   6 tablespoons water
   *2 cups tomato juice (cooked down to 1 cup
      tomato sauce)
   1 cup cooked French-style green beans, diced
   4 ounces canned mushrooms, cut up

In small saucepan, combine green pepper, celery, onion, liquid from
canned mushrooms, chicken broth powder and water and cook about
15 mintues. Add tomato sauce, green beans and mushrooms; heat
and serve.
   Keep a jar of this in your refrigerator at all times and serve over
cooked vegetables. Very good with cooked cabbage. Served over

   * *Limited food—see Menu Plan, p. 18-20, for legal amount.*

cooked bean sprouts, it "becomes" "Spaghetti and Creole Sauce W.W." Sometimes chopped parsley may be added. Use also for scrambled eggs, as filling for omelet, as sauce over broiled or barbecued chicken, fish, cheese, soufflés, etc.

CUCUMBER-LEMON SAUCE, BLENDER STYLE

> 2 medium cucumbers, sliced, salted, but not peeled
> Juice of ½ lemon
> ¼ teaspoon paprika
> 1 teaspoon salt

Place in blender and purée until smooth. Serve cold. Excellent with fish. May be combined with Sour Cream W.W. Style and served over varied vegetables.

CUCUMBER SAUCE

Chop a large peeled cucumber. Drain well. Add 2 tablespoons vinegar, salt, pepper. Mix well. Chill and serve over cold tuna, salmon, or other fish.

CURRY SAUCE FOR SLICED FRUIT, COLD CHICKEN OR FISH

> 4 stalks celery, diced
> 1 large green pepper, diced
> 1 large red pepper, diced
> Onion flavor (salt or dehydrated onion flakes)
> 2 cups strong chicken broth
> *4 tablespoons bread crumbs (make from half
>   slice of bread)
> Curry powder to taste

Cook the vegetables, covered with chicken broth, in a saucepan until they have cooked away almost to nothing but have not browned. Stir in 4 tablespoons bread crumbs. Serve hot sauce over cold sliced eggs, chicken or fish, which makes a pleasant, good combination.

Note: Since bread is allowed only at breakfast or luncheon, you may not use this sauce, if thickened, at dinner. However, it may be used without thickening at any time.

CHINESE SWEET AND SOUR SAUCE

> 5 tablespoons lemon juice
> ¾ cup water
> 1 tablespoon soy sauce
> 1 clove of garlic, cut in several places so essence
>   can be extracted quickly
> 1 teaspoon sugar substitute
> 1 2-inch square of pimento, finely diced

In saucepan, combine all ingredients. Cook for 10 minutes, uncovered. Discard garlic. Use for fruit salad, with Chinese dishes as substitute for Duck Sauce, chutney, etc. A good sauce for your basic inventory, it is also unlimited. Note: You may use tomato juice to replace part of the water, but tomato juice must be counted as daily intake is limited to 12 ounces.

SWEET AND SOUR PINEAPPLE SAUCE

Add *⅛ pineapple, cut into very fine dice, to Chinese Sweet and Sour Sauce, and ¼ teaspoon sugar substitute. Cook until thickened. Note: Count pineapple as ½ fruit.

* Limited food—see Menu Plan, p. 18-20, for legal amount.

DILL CREAM DRESSING

> *1 pound cottage cheese
> *3 tablespoons buttermilk
> 2 teaspoons fresh chopped dill (or ½ teaspoon
>   dried)

Combine all ingredients in a blender and purée until smooth. Excellent as a dressing over salad greens (a variety of them) for luncheon. The cottage cheese in this recipe will serve 4 at luncheon. It can also be divided to serve 8, but in that case add half a portion of luncheon eggs, fish, meat, or poultry for each serving.

DILL MARINADE FOR SHRIMP, CHICKEN, ETC.

> 1 packet instant chicken broth mix
> 1 cup water
> 4 cloves fresh garlic, cut up
> Fresh dill
> Soy sauce

Combine in saucepan, heat quickly and use to marinate fish and poultry.

FINES HERBES

Cook 2 tablespoons dehydrated onion flakes in 2 tablespoons wine vinegar and 3 tablespoons chicken stock. When onions are cooked—five minutes—strain and add to liquid 1 teaspoon each fine chopped parsley and chives, salt and freshly ground pepper. Flavor with artificial butter seasoning. Serve very hot over broiled fish.

FISH SAUCE OR ESSENCE

Cook fish stock (see index for recipe) until it is greatly reduced, to an "essence." Serve as a sauce or use in making sauces for fish. Stems from mushrooms are often added to the stock before it is reduced, and the stock strained.

FRUIT SALAD DRESSING

    4 tablespoons lemon juice
    4 tablespoons non-caloric ginger ale
  *½ cup orange juice
    ¼ teaspoon sugar substitute
    Few drops of peppermint extract
    Few drops of green coloring

Put all ingredients into blender container, and whirl them at high speed for a few seconds. Serve over cut-up fruits: ¼ pineapple, segments of half a grapefruit and a small apple make a good combination, to be served to 4. (Orange juice counts as 1 fruit.)

GARLIC SAUCE

    2 cloves garlic
  *¼ cup tomato sauce (tomato juice boiled down
      to half its volume)
    ¼ cup vinegar
    1 tablespoon Worcestershire sauce
    1 teaspoon paprika
    ½ teaspoon dry mustard
    2 drops Tabasco sauce

Blend about 20 seconds. Good as baste when barbecuing steak or hamburgers.

GARLIC VINEGAR

> 1 cup mild vinegar
> 4 cloves garlic, peeled and halved

Heat vinegar to boiling. Remove from heat, add garlic and cool. Remove garlic. Store in stoppered bottles. Use as marinade for cooked diced or shredded beets.

GARLIC TOMATO JUICE DRESSING

> 1 teaspoon onion flakes
> 1 teaspoon salt
> *½ cup tomato juice
> 2 tablespoons lemon juice or vinegar
> ½ teaspoon mustard
> 2 cloves garlic, crushed to a pulp

Mix all ingredients in a bowl. Store covered in refrigerator. Shake well before using.

GOLDEN DRESSING

> *1 egg slightly beaten
> *¼ cup orange juice
> ¼ cup lemon juice
> ½ teaspoon liquid sugar substitute

Combine all ingredients in small saucepan and cook for a few minutes over very low direct heat, or place over boiling water in double boiler. Stir constantly until mixture thickens. Use over fruit salad. Excellent with a jellied salad.

 * *Limited food—see Menu Plan, p. 18-20, for legal amount.*

ITALIAN-STYLE GRAVY W.W.

> *12 ounces tomato juice
> 1 cup cooked mushrooms (fresh or canned)
> ¼ cup dehydrated onion flakes, soaked in water
> 1 large green pepper
> 1 can asparagus
> 1 ounce wine vinegar
> Garlic (if desired)
> Salt
> Pepper
> Thyme or parsley flakes

Blend all ingredients in blender, or chop very fine. Steam in pot until thick as gravy, about ½ hour. Store in refrigerator. May be used over cooked fish or vegetables, with browned chicken to make Chicken Cacciatore, with browned veal cubes to make **Veal Scallopine**, used as a ketchup over meat, etc.

GREEN GODDESS DRESSING W.W.

> 4 tablespoons tarragon vinegar
> 1 tablespoon lemon juice
> ¼ cup chopped chives
> 2 large cloves garlic, put through press or mashed
>   fine
> *1 cup Sour Cream W.W.
> ⅓ cup finely chopped parsley
> Freshly grated pepper

Boil vinegar about 20 minutes until it is reduced one-half. Let cool. Combine with other ingredients, mix well, and refrigerate until ready to use. Serve over mixed greens, using at least 3 different kinds of lettuce—iceberg, chicory, romaine, escarole, etc.—and you will have a most refreshing luncheon salad.

QUICK ITALIAN TOMATO SAUCE

¼ cup dehydrated onion flakes, diced and soaked
   in water
1 green pepper, diced
1 clove garlic
*1 cup tomato juice, cooked until it is reduced to
   half its volume
Salt
Pepper
Dried oregano or basil

Heat a heavy skillet, add onion and green pepper and let brown
lightly, stirring to prevent burning. Add other ingredients and cook
for 15 minutes. Serve with bean sprouts to make "Spaghetti with
Italian Tomato Sauce."

MARINADE FOR LAMB

Combine lime juice and water in equal amounts (1 tablespoon each), 1 teaspoon soy sauce, 1 crushed clove garlic, and ½ teaspoon onion salt. Brush over lamb and let stand overnight. Then broil or roast.

MINT SAUCE

¼ cup chopped mint leaves, ½ cup mild vinegar and ½ teaspoon sugar substitute make a nice sauce. Let stand for half an hour. Can also be puréed in blender. Nice with lamb.

HEALTHADE

    ¼ cup liquid from any cooked green or yellow
       vegetable
    ½ cup fresh lemon juice (or ¼ cup each lemon
       juice and vinegar)
    2 teaspoons onion juice
    1 clove garlic
    1 teaspoon salt
    ⅛ teaspoon pepper
    ¼ teaspoon paprika
    2 teaspoons parsley

Combine all ingredients and bring to a boil. Chill before serving.

FRESH MUSHROOM SAUCE

Quickly wash mushrooms. Slice large ones lengthwise in quarters, cut small ones in half. Sprinkle with lemon juice (optional) and cook for 5 minutes in stock, consommé, or water which barely covers them. Most of stock should boil down. Season well and serve hot.

Note: If you are using this sauce at luncheon, you may thicken it by adding *bread crumbs made from half a slice of luncheon bread, whirred in blender.

Delicious Mushroom Sauce

quickly wash mushrooms.

Lemon juice optional

Cut mushrooms in quarters or halves

Cook for five minutes

Season and serve hot.

ANOTHER IDEA FOR USING MUSHROOMS

Make mushroom ketchup: Chop coarsely 1 pound mushrooms, sprinkle with 1 tablespoon salt; let stand overnight. Add 2 tablespoons vinegar, ½ teaspoon onion flakes, a dash of grated horseradish, allspice, ground cloves and cayenne pepper. Bring mixture to boil. Simmer for half an hour, stirring often. Purée through fine sieve or in blender. (If ketchup is too thick, thin with vinegar.) Bring to boil, turn off heat, and refrigerate in jar; or pour into hot sterilized jars and seal.

MUSTARD DRESSING (For Shredded Cabbage)

    1 tablespoon prepared mustard
    2 tablespoons lemon juice
    Dash cayenne pepper
 *⅔ cup non-fat skim milk powder
    ⅔ cup water
    ½ teaspoon salt
    Dash freshly grated pepper
    ½ teaspoon sugar substitute

Refrigerate ingredients in mixing bowl, chill and whip with electric
mixer until quite thick. (Combine with 3 cups shredded cabbage,
3 tablespoons chopped celery, and 3 tablespoons diced green pepper.)

  Note: Count skim milk powder as total of 2 cups skim milk.
Everything else is unlimited.

ONION SAUCE

    2 tablespoons dehydrated onion flakes
 *3 tablespoons skim milk
 *½ cup bread crumbs (made from 1 slice of
      luncheon bread puréed in blender)

Cook the dehydrated onion flakes in the skim milk for 5 minutes.
When onion is soft, strain milk, discard onion, and add bread
crumbs to make a thick sauce. Serve at luncheon over a weighed
portion of cooked chicken, turkey or fish, or over an unlimited
vegetable such as cooked mushrooms, asparagus, etc.

SIMPLE PARSLEY SAUCE FOR FISH

Combine minced parsley with lemon juice and pour over baked or
broiled fish on serving platter.

BLENDER LEMON-PARSLEY SAUCE

½ cup parsley sprigs
1 teaspoon dehydrated onion flakes, soaked in hot
    water for 5 minutes
1 lemon, peeled, seeded and quartered
½ teaspoon salt

Put all ingredients into blender and process until smooth. Brush on
fish while baking or broiling. Or use on lamb chops. Unlimited.

PIMENTO FRENCH DRESSING

½ teaspoon dry mustard
½ teaspoon paprika
½ teaspoon salt
¼ teaspoon pepper
¼ cup lemon juice and wine vinegar combined
⅔ cup chicken or beef stock
1 clove garlic, crushed
3 tablespoons pimento
¼ teaspoon sugar substitute
¼ teaspoon artificial butter flavor

Put all ingredients into blender container and let whiz around
until well puréed. To make without a blender, mash pimento, combine with other ingredients in a jar, and store. Shake before using.
A good basic dressing to have on hand at all times.

BASIL PIMENTO DRESSING

Use Pimento French Dressing, to which add 1 teaspoon dried basil
leaves, or 1 tablespoon chopped fresh leaves. Let steep several hours
before using.

PIMENTO SAUCE

    4 ounces roasted pimentos
    1 tablespoon pimento liquid or water
  *1 tablespoon nonfat dry milk solids
    Salt and pepper to taste

Put pimentos, liquid, milk solids, and salt and pepper into the blender container and whiz until well puréed. Serve with fish or eggs. Also a great success over cooked cauliflower.

REMOULADE SAUCE

  *1 recipe Sauce Chambord (see index)
    2 tablespoons chopped gherkins
    2 tablespoons chopped capers
    2 teaspoons chopped chives
  *1 hard-cooked egg, chopped
    2 tablespoons finely chopped parsley
    2 tablespoons finely chopped tarragon

To 1 recipe Sauce Chambord add chopped gherkins, capers, chives, hard-boiled egg, parsley and tarragon. Serve over tuna fish, crab meat, lobster, etc. Note: Egg may be omitted.

DEEP-SOUTH DINNER

  Okra Soup (Chicken Gumbo), p. 193
  Bowl of Cooked Cleaned Shrimp (legal weight)
  Rémoulade Sauce (made without egg)
  Hot Spinach Salad, p. 177
    or *Old Virginia Tomato Aspic,* p. 204
  Ginger Melon Mold, p. 255

SOUR CREAM W.W.

*⅔ cup cottage cheese
¼ cup water
¼ teaspoon salt (optional)
1 teaspoon lemon juice

Put into blender container and blend until free from all lumps. If necessary, use a rubber spatula to turn cheese from sides of container into center where blades can get to it. Makes about 1 cup. Store in cheese carton if convenient. Use slightly less or more water depending on desired thickness.

VARIATIONS:

1. Sweeten with 1 teaspoon granulated sugar substitute. Add 3 tablespoons lemon juice and a dash of ginger. Taste and add more ginger if you wish. Mint leaves are a nice addition too. Use over fresh fruit cup.
2. Add chopped or grated cucumbers, minced parsley, radishes, and tarragon vinegar. Serve over tuna fish salad or cold cooked French-style green beans. Watch count, following your Menu Plan.

QUICK TANGY DRESSING

2 tablespoons dehydrated onion flakes
*½ cup tomato sauce (1 cup tomato juice cooked
    down to half its volume)
1 teaspoon Worcestershire sauce
3 tablespoons lemon juice
Dash of celery salt

Combine all ingredients in blender container and whip until smooth.

* *Limited food—see Menu Plan, p. 18-20, for legal amount.*

SEA FOOD COCKTAIL SAUCE

*½ cup tomato sauce (1 cup tomato juice cooked
    down to half its volume)
1 teaspoon horseradish sauce
1 teaspoon lemon juice
½ teaspoon Worcestershire sauce
½ teaspoon salt
Any other seasoning desired:
    Tabasco sauce makes it hot

Mix ingredients and serve with shrimp or other cooked seafood. For a creamier cocktail sauce, purée in blender. A thicker sauce may be made as follows:

For luncheon—by adding *bread crumbs made from a slice of bread whizzed in blender.

For dinner—by adding mashed *whole tomato. However, tomato is a limited vegetables and dinner allowance would have to be reduced accordingly, depending on the amount of Cocktail Sauce you use.

SOY SAUCE

Try adding soy sauce to one of the salad dressings. You'll get a completely new flavor. Soy sauce is a favorite ingredient with Weight Watchers, judging by the number of times it is included in recipes brought in by our members.

SPICY SALAD DRESSING

1 medium stalk celery
¼ green pepper
½ teaspoon onion salt
½ teaspoon salt
Sugar substitute to taste
½ cup vinegar
1 drop Tabasco sauce

Grind both vegetables together. Mix salts, sugar substitute, vinegar and Tabasco. Shake well. Combine with vegetables. Yields ¾ cup.

TOMATO FRENCH DRESSING

> *½ cup tomato juice
> 2 tablespoons vinegar
> 2 tablespoons finely chopped green pepper (the frozen variety is fine)
> ½-1 teaspoon Worcestershire sauce
> ½ teaspoon salt
> ½ teaspoon dry mustard
> 1 clove garlic or garlic salt
> ¼ teaspoon liquid sugar substitute

Combine all ingredients in blender and purée. Good with salad or cold meats. This is a basic sauce and should be in your refrigerator at all times. It thickens and improves as it stands. Everything is unlimited (tomato juice is "unlimited" to the extent of 12 ounces daily).

TOMATO FRENCH DRESSING WITH ONION

To the above dressing, add 1 teaspoon dehydrated onion flakes which have been soaked in hot water for 5 minutes. Include the water.

CREAMY TOMATO DRESSING

Add *1 tablespoon nonfat dry milk powder to Tomato French Dressing before blending.

THOUSAND ISLAND DRESSING

After removing Tomato French Dressing from the blender, add ¼ cup finely diced green pepper, 3 tablespoons finely diced dill pickles or pickle relish, 3 tablespoons finely diced pimento and 2 teaspoons finely minced parsley. Store in refrigerator and use as needed. Excellent over hearts of lettuce.

TOMATO SAUCE

Cook *tomato juice until it is reduced one-half (45-60 minutes). Season to taste with salt and pepper. Result—a delicious tomato sauce.

WATER-CRESS SALAD DRESSING

   ⅓ cup lemon juice
 *½ cup tomato sauce (1 cup tomato juice cooked
      down to half its volume)
   Salt
   1 cup chopped water cress

Mix ingredients. Serve over plain greens, sliced tomatoes, or with tuna fish.

WEIGHT WATCHERS DIP FOR VEGETABLES

   1 teaspoon Worcestershire sauce
   Dash Tabasco sauce
 *6 ounces cottage cheese
   1 4-ounce can pimentos, drained (½ cup)
   ⅛ teaspoon salt
   ⅛ teaspoon garlic salt

Place in a blender and purée until smooth. (You may substitute parsley, chopped very fine, for pimentos.) Serve as dip for sticks of fresh vegetables including celery, crisp young string beans, and small leaves of endive.

SUMMER LUNCHEON FOR TWO

Chilled Tomato Juice
   Hang a slice of lemon over the glass
2 Open Sandwiches of White Turkey
   Each made from 2 ounces of meat on toast
Fresh Unlimited Vegetables, W.W. Dip
Fruit Gelatin, Whipped Topping

TWO DRESSINGS AD LIB

At various times, members of Weight Watchers bring in their recipes for salad dressings using the ingredients listed below. Each member seems to use a slightly different proportion, so we have decided to list them all, and let you mix them to your own taste and following your own method. Some use a blender, some shake it in a jar.

#1 DRESSING

Vinegar
Oregano
Salt
Garlic
Pepper
Sugar substitute
Dry mustard
Paprika
Tomato juice
Soy sauce

#2 DRESSING

Buttermilk
Varied herbs (basil, tarragon)
Garlic
Vinegar or lemon

RULES FOR USING FRUIT

Select one Vitamin C fruit—orange or grapefruit—each day. Otherwise, vary selections. Fruits may be eaten raw or cooked. One-half cup equals 1 fruit, except where otherwise marked.

½ small cantaloupe = 1 fruit
2-inch wedge honeydew melon = 1 fruit
¼ medium pineapple = 1 fruit
1 medium apple = 1 fruit

No bananas, cherries, dried fruits, grapes, watermelon.

> WOMEN: 3 fruits daily
> MEN: 5 fruits daily
> TEENAGERS: 5 fruits daily

COLA LIBRA

> 1 cup non-caloric cola soda
> ¼ teaspoon angostura bitters
> Dash lemon juice (optional)

Combine ingredients, shake or stir and serve over ice.

GINGER-MINT COOLER

> 1 cup water
> 1 tablespoon liquid sugar substitute
> ¼ cup chopped mint leaves
> ½ cup lemon juice
> *2 cups orange juice
> 1 quart non-caloric ginger ale

Combine water, sugar substitute and mint; bring to a boil. Strain and cool. At serving time, add remaining ingredients. Pour over finely crushed ice in tall glasses. Makes 8 servings. Count each as ½ fruit.

CRYSTAL GELATIN

> 1 package unflavored gelatin
> 16 ounces any flavor non-caloric carbonated soda

Sprinkle gelatin over ¼ cup carbonated soda to soften, and set aside. Heat remaining soda, combine with gelatin, stirring to dissolve gelatin. Pour into glass serving dishes and refrigerate until jelled. Serve cut into cubes if desired. *Whipped topping may be added if you wish.

BUTTERMILK FRUIT SALAD

    1 envelope unflavored gelatin
    ¼ cup water
    1 tablespoon liquid sugar substitute
    1 tablespoon lemon juice
  *1¼ cups buttermilk
    1 teaspoon almond extract
  *1 cup cut-up peaches, apples or other legal fresh fruits

Soften gelatin in ¼ cup cold water. Place over low heat and stir until gelatin is dissolved. Add sugar substitute, lemon juice, buttermilk and almond extract. Chill until mixture begins to thicken. Fold in fruit. Put into a wet mold. Chill until firm. Unmold on greens. 4 servings; each serving counts as ½ fruit, 5 tablespoons buttermilk.

CALIFORNIA GARDEN SALAD

  *¼ grapefruit, peeled and sliced thin
  *½ navel orange, peeled and sliced thin
    2 large rings of green pepper
    Lettuce, torn into pieces
  *⅓ cup cottage cheese
  *Sour Cream W.W. (see index for recipe), made
      from ⅓ cup cottage cheese

Remove seeds from grapefruit and orange slices and arrange them, with pepper rings, in a circle on a bed of lettuce. Put a ball of cottage cheese in the center. Chill before serving. Makes 1 salad, counting as 1 fruit and 6 ounces cheese.

FRUIT SALAD

Combine *¼ apple, *¼ peeled orange and *⅛ peeled grapefruit, all cut in dice with *2 tablespoons raspberries. Arrange on crisp lettuce leaves and serve with *Whipped Topping. (See index for recipe for Whipped Topping, and count skim milk according to the amount used.)

GOLDEN GLOW SALAD

      2 envelopes unflavored gelatin
    *3 cups grapefruit and orange sections (save juices)
      2 cups boiling water
      ½ cup lemon juice
      2 tablespoons liquid sugar substitute
      4 teaspoons vinegar
      ½ teaspoon salt
      2 cups grated cabbage

Soften gelatin in juice drained from grapefruit and orange sections; add boiling water, stirring to dissolve gelatin. Add lemon juice, sugar substitute, vinegar and salt; chill until mixture begins to thicken. Fold in grapefruit sections and grated cabbage. Spoon into a wet 2-quart mold. Chill until firm. To serve, unmold on a bed of crisp chilled salad greens. Make 12 servings. Each serving counts as ½ fruit.

SALAD A LA RITZ

    *1 apple, diced
    *½ pineapple, diced
     1 green pepper, diced
    *½ grapefruit, diced

Arrange on water cress large dices of apple, pineapple, green pepper and grapefruit. Chill before serving. Pass a small pitcher of Cucumber-Lemon Sauce or Chinese Sweet and Sour Sauce (see index for recipe).

Ever think of cutting unpeeled *apples or *oranges in rings, then in half again, and using the results as dippers? For seasoned *Sour Cream W.W. maybe? Good! But don't forget to count the fruit—and Sour Cream.

RED AND GREEN SALAD

Combine equal amounts of chopped celery, pimento, shredded green pepper and *grapefruit sections. Serve over endive with Chinese Sweet and Sour Sauce (see index for recipe). Count fruit according to amount used.

MIXED LUNCHEON SALAD

   3 tablespoons chopped pimento
   3 tablespoons chopped green pepper
 *½ cup grapefruit sections
 *⅓ cup cottage cheese
 *Sour Cream W.W. made from ⅓ cup cottage
      cheese and water (see index for recipe)

Combine ingredients and serve on lettuce bed. Count as 1 luncheon allowance cottage cheese; 1 fruit.

FRUIT GELATIN

Follow Lemon Gelatin recipe (see index for page number) but let gelatin cool in refrigerator until it is the consistency of syrup. Then fold in *fruit. (Count fruit in daily intake.)

Note: If you have allowed the gelatin to become too stiff to fold in fruit, place mold containing it in a bowl of hot water and stir until gelatin is liquid. Then chill again to syrup stage.

FRUIT TOPPING FOR FRENCH TOAST

Mash *½ cup berries or cooked fruit, sprinkle with sugar substitute and serve as sauce for French toast. Count as 1 fruit.

FLORIDA SALAD

Combine *2 cups grapefruit sections with ¼ cup chopped green pepper, ¼ cup chopped pimentos and *1 cup peeled and cubed apples. Serve with Fruit Salad Dressing W.W. in orange or grapefruit shells. The fruit totals 3 cups; a standard fruit serving is ½ cup; therefore this makes 6 salads, each counting as 1 fruit.

APPLE, ORANGE AND ONION SALAD

    *1 orange
    *1 tart eating apple
     ½ large green pepper
    *½ sweet onion
     Chives or parsley sprigs

Peel and slice in more or less matching circles the orange, apple (sprinkled with lemon juice so it does not discolor), pepper (from which seeds and membranes are removed) and a half sweet onion. Arrange on crisp lettuce in overlapping rings, a slice each of orange, onion, apple, and green pepper. Sprinkle with finely cut chives or parsley sprigs and serve for dinner salad with French Dressing W.W. Serves 2; each serving uses 1 allowed fruit and ¼ limited vegetable.

SALAD OF APPLE AND CHEESE BALLS

  *1 apple, finely chopped
   ¼ cup finely chopped celery
  *⅓ cup cottage cheese
   1 tablespoon finely chopped pimentos
  *Sour Cream W.W. (made from ⅓ cup cottage
     cheese and water)

Combine apple, celery, cottage cheese (mashed as smooth as possible), and chopped pimentos. Mix thoroughly with fork. Roll into small balls (about 1 inch in diameter). Serve on crisp romaine leaves with rings of green pepper as topping. Use with Sour Cream W.W. (see index for recipe). Count as luncheon allowance of cheese and 1 fruit.

APPLE SNOW

  *1 cup Applesauce W.W., chilled
  *1 cup Whipped Topping W.W., chilled

Just before serving, fold applesauce into topping. Spoon into cups. Sprinkle with cinnamon. Two servings. (Recipe equals 2 fruits and 1 glass milk.)

APPLES AND SAUERKRAUT

  *4 tart apples
   2 cups sauerkraut
   Salt
   Pepper
   Caraway seed

Peel apples, discard cores, and cut fruit into slices. Arrange in casserole with layers of sauerkraut seasoned with salt, pepper and caraway seed. Pour in 6 tablespoons sauerkraut juice or water. Bake in moderate or hot oven 35 minutes or until apples are done. Makes a good accompaniment for meat. Can be stored for about a week. 4 servings. 1 serving equals 1 fruit.

APPLE, CELERY AND BEET SALAD

> ¾ cup diced celery stalks
> *2 eating apples, cut into large dice
> *¼ cup grated beets

Peel, core and cube apples. Combine with celery and beets. Mix with French Dressing W.W. and serve on crisp water cress. Four servings; each serving counts as ½ fruit.

Note: Beets are a limited vegetable and this salad may be used only at dinner.

APPLE MIX

Combine equal amount of crisp shredded lettuce and shredded red cabbage for use as salad base. Cut *apple slices rather large, and add an equal amount of *peach slices and *tangerine sections. Allow ½ cup for each portion. Measure fruit before adding dressing. Serve with Chinese Sweet and Sour Sauce (see index for recipe).

APPLE CHARLOTTE

> *1 slice stale white bread
> *½ cup Applesauce W.W.
> Artificial butter flavor
> Granulated sugar substitute and cinnamon mixture

Cut stale white bread from luncheon allowance into halves. Cut one half into thin strips, or make into bread crumbs, and use to line bottom of small casserole. Add Applesauce W.W. seasoned with artificial butter flavor. Top with crumbs made from second half of bread. Sprinkle with sugar substitute and cinnamon and bake uncovered in moderate or hot oven until top of bread is brown.

Apples bake well in low, hot or moderate ovens. You may put apples in oven along with other foods.

core 4 apples

peel apples leaving skin on lower half.

bake in individual casserole

pour in non-caloric beverage.

Note: for a refreshing change pour buttermilk over apples before serving. May be served hot or cold.

* Limited food—see Menu Plan, p. 18-20, for legal amount.

BAKED APPLES

Apples bake equally well in low, hot, or moderate ovens, so set the oven temperature according to the needs of other dishes in your meal. Cinnamon, nutmeg and lemon juice are all good flavorings for apples.

   *Baking apples
   Dash cinnamon
   2 packets granulated sugar substitute
   Non-caloric carbonated soda (black cherry,
      raspberry, lemon, etc.)

Wash and core apples. Cut off peel ⅓ of the way down. Place each apple in an individual casserole or custard cup. Combine cinnamon, sugar substitute and non-caloric soda and pour over apples (should be almost halfway up). Bake in moderate oven at 375°F. until apples are tender and juicy, about 50 minutes. Serve warm or cold.

*Buttermilk served over baked apples—a refreshing change.

CURRIED BAKED APPLES

Combine 2 teaspoons curry powder (or to taste) with ginger ale or other non-caloric carbonated drink and put over baking *apples before putting into oven.

APPLESAUCE FOR ONE

   *1 cut-up apple, red skin left on
   ⅓ cup water
   Liquid sugar substitute to taste

Combine apple and water in blender and blend for no more than half a minute. Pour into saucepan, cover and bring to boil. Cook 2 minutes. Cool slightly, then sweeten to taste with liquid sugar substitute. Makes ½ cup; 1 serving. (Note: Non-caloric carbonated soda could be used in place of water.)

APPLESAUCE W. W.

*8 apples (about 2 pounds) quartered
½ cup water
1 tablespoon liquid sugar substitute
1 tablespoon lemon juice

Combine apples and water in saucepan; cover and simmer 15 to 20 minutes, or until tender. Force through food mill. Add sugar substitute and lemon juice, mixing well. A drop of artificial butter flavor may be added. Chill and refrigerate to use as allowed. Makes 8 servings.

BAKED APPLE AND PINEAPPLE

*6 cooking apples
*1 small pineapple, cut into thin wedges
1 cup black cherry non-caloric carbonated soda
3 teaspoons lemon juice
1 teaspoon liquid sugar substitute
¼ teaspoon cinnamon

Wash and core apples. Place in large baking dish or cake pan. Peel and slice pineapple, cut into 3-inch wedges, and place in pan with apples. Add rest of ingredients and bake at 350°-400° until pineapple is cooked and apples are very soft. Allow to cool in baking pan so liquid can be absorbed into fruit. This makes a delicious dessert or bedtime snack topped with allowed portion of *Whipped Topping W.W. May be stored in the refrigerator for about a week. Ten servings.

Company theme: Bake this in round casserole. Save the top of pineapple and just before serving set it in center of casserole.

Note: Either fruit can be prepared separately following this recipe if preferred.

GRAPE WHIP

> 2 cups black cherry or any flavor non-caloric
>   carbonated beverage
> 1 package unflavored gelatin
> *Whipped Topping (see index for recipe)

Soften gelatin by sprinkling it on ½ cup non-caloric carbonated grape soda pop in double boiler. Stir over hot water to dissolve gelatin. Remove from heat and add remaining beverage. Stir well. Pour into four champagne goblets. Refrigerate until firm. Serve with Whipped Topping. (Unlimited if served without Whipped Topping.)

BLACK CHERRY GELATIN WHIP

> 1 envelope unflavored gelatin
> 1½ cups non-caloric black cherry carbonated soda
> 2 teaspoons lemon juice
> 1 teaspoon liquid sugar substitute
> *½ cup evaporated skim milk, very cold
> ½ teaspoon unflavored gelatin
> ½ teaspoon vanilla

Soften gelatin in ½ cup cherry soda. Bring to boil remaining cup of cherry soda. Mix with gelatin, lemon juice and sugar substitute and refrigerate until almost set. Beat skim milk with rotary or electric beater until it stands in peaks. Slowly add gelatin mixture. Beat 1 minute more. Place in gelatin mold or individual custard cups and chill. Should be eaten same day as prepared as some separation occurs when allowed to stay overnight.

CHILLED CRANBERRY COCKTAIL

* *1 cup cranberries
* 2 cups water
* *1 cup orange juice
* 2 tablespoons lemon juice
* 1 tablespoon liquid sugar substitute

Combine cranberries and water; cook until skins pop. Place in blender and blend 1 minute. Strain and add remaining ingredients. Chill before serving. Makes 4 servings, 1 fruit each.

JELLIED CRANBERRY SAUCE

* *2 cups raw cranberries
* 1 cup water
* 1 envelope gelatin
* ¼ cup cold water
* 1½ tablespoons liquid sugar substitute (or to taste)

Combine cranberries and the 1 cup water; cook until skins pop. Soften gelatin in the ¼ cup cold water. Add cooked cranberries, stirring to dissolve gelatin. Add liquid sugar substitute. Pour into a 1-pound can, or 2-cup mold. Chill until set. Slice to serve.

To make plain cranberry jelly, force cooked cranberries through food mill or strainer; add to softened gelatin and proceed as above. 4 servings, 1 fruit per serving.

* Limited food—see Menu Plan, p. 18-20, for legal amount.

BROILED GRAPEFRUIT

In my opinion a half *grapefruit is most refreshing and delicious when served chilled. But in winter especially many people like it better when heated. Be my guest!

Cut grapefruit in half and use knife to free the segments. Cut out core. Sprinkle a few drops liquid sugar substitute over grapefruit halves and broil until edges are pale gold. Serve hot.

GRAPEFRUIT COCKTAIL

Sprinkle *grapefruit sections with sugar subtitute, then roll in finely chopped mint leaves. Serve in chilled sherbet glass with more mint.

KUMQUATS

Cover 1 quart *kumquats in water. Bring to boil, drain, and cover with fresh water. Repeat this twice more so that kumquats have been boiled in 3 different waters to remove bitterness. Let kumquats cook in third water until they are soft and most of liquid has boiled away. Add sugar substitute (about ¼ cup) and taste to adjust seasoning. Serves as garnish for fish or meat platter. Count ½ cup as 1 fruit. Also delicious sliced very thin for salads or as a topping for Ice Cream W.W. (see index for recipe).

LEMON GELATIN

 1 envelope unflavored gelatin
 ¾ cup cold water
 Dash of salt
 2 teaspoons liquid sugar substitute
 ⅓ cup lemon or lime juice

Sprinkle gelatin over cold water in saucepan. Heat over low flame, stirring constantly. Add a dash of salt, liquid sugar substitute, lemon or lime juice. Mix by stirring. Pour into individual wet molds and chill until firm. Serve with W.W. Whipped Topping if you wish. Unlimited.

LEMON ICE

> 1 envelope unflavored gelatin
> 1 cup cold water
> Rind of 1 lemon
> ¼ cup lemon juice
> 1½ teaspoons liquid sugar substitute
> *2 egg whites
> Pinch salt

Soften gelatin in ¼ cup cold water in saucepan and dissolve over low heat. Peel the yellow rind of lemon, removing all of the inside white membrane. Put dissolved gelatin, lemon rind, lemon juice and liquid sugar substitute in blender and blend until the rind is cut fine. Chill mixture to thicken it. Meanwhile beat egg whites and salt with rotary egg beater (not in blender) until stiff but not dry. Fold lemon mixture into egg whites. Pour into tray of freezer and freeze as quickly as possible (freezer should be at coldest setting). When mixture has frozen about 1 inch from edge, remove it to a bowl and whip with egg beater until it is the consistency of mashed potatoes; do not overbeat it. Freeze again in freezer pan until firm. Makes 4 half-cup servings; use for luncheon.

Note: As this dessert uses only egg whites, it must be combined with a dish that includes egg yolks. (Beaten egg yolks thinned with *skim milk or water make good scrambled eggs.)

Happiness is seeing your new reflection in a full-length mirror.

* *Limited food—see Menu Plan, p. 18-20, for legal amount.*

LEMONADE

>   2 packets granulated sugar substitute
>   2 tablespoons strained fresh or reconstituted
>   lemon juice
>   1 cup water
>   Ice
>   1 lemon slice

Mix first three ingredients and serve over ice in large glass. Make a slit in lemon slice and hang it on glass. Washed mint leaves may be floated on top. Makes 1 serving.

MINTED MELON

>   1 cup non-caloric lemon-lime carbonated beverage
>   ¼ teaspoon mint extract
>   *6 halves of cantaloupe (seeds removed)

Combine carbonated beverage and mint leaves. Pour onto melon. Chill. Makes 6 servings.

MINTED HONEYDEW AND PEAR COMPOTE

>   *1 cup fresh ripe pear slices
>   *1 cup honeydew melon balls
>   ⅓ cup lemon juice
>   2 teaspoons liquid sugar substitute (or to taste)
>   1 tablespoon chopped mint leaves

Combine all ingredients and mix well. Spoon into compote or sherbet glasses. Chill for 3 to 4 hours before serving. Garnish with fresh mint. Makes 4 servings. Count each serving as 1 fruit. Note: Honeydew melon balls can be cut with small end of melon ball scoop.

GINGER MELON MOLD

    2 envelopes unflavored gelatin
    ½ cup lemon juice
    ½ cup boiling water
    2 tablespoons liquid sugar substitute
    2 cups non-caloric ginger ale
  *1½ cups honeydew melon balls, sprinkled lightly
      with ground ginger

Soften gelatin in lemon juice; add boiling water, stirring to dissolve.
Add liquid sugar substitute and ginger ale; chill until mixture begins
to thicken. Add honeydew melon balls, and pour into a 1-quart mold.
Chill until set. To serve, unmold and garnish with mint, if desired.
Makes 6 servings; count each serving as ½ fruit.

LIME-MELON MOLD

    1 envelope unflavored gelatin
    ¼ cup cold water
    1 cup hot water
    ½ cup lime juice
    2¼ teaspoons sugar substitute
    Dash of salt
  *2 cups small melon balls

Soften gelatin over cold water; add hot water to dissolve gelatin.
Stir in lime juice, sugar substitute and salt. Chill until syrupy. Fold
in melon balls. Spoon into 1 quart mold or 4 individual molds. Chill
until firm. A border of mint leaves or water cress placed around un-
molded gelatin is an attractive contrast. Makes 4 servings; each one
has 1 full fruit.

  * *Limited food—see Menu Plan, p. 18-20, for legal amount.*

NECTARINE BUTTERMILK SHERBET

    1 package plain gelatin
    2 tablespoons cold water
    ¼ cup hot water
    ¼ teaspoon rum flavor
    ¼ teaspoon artificial butter flavor
    1½ teaspoons liquid sugar substitute
    *2 ripe nectarines
    *1 cup buttermilk

Sprinkle gelatin over cold water to soften it, then dissolve in hot water. Place in blender with remaining ingredients and blend for a few seconds. Pour into custard cups and chill about 1 hour or until set. Serves 2; count 1 fruit and ½ cup milk for each serving.

ORANGE GELATIN DESSERT

    1 envelope unflavored gelatin
    ½ cup cold water
    6 packets granulated sugar substitute
    ⅛ teaspoon salt
    ⅔ cup hot water
    *½ cup orange juice

Soften gelatin in water; stir in sugar substitute, salt, and hot water until gelatin is dissolved. Stir in orange juice. Pour ¾ cup into each of two individual molds. Refrigerate until set. Makes 2 servings. Count each one as ½ fruit.

ORANGE DELIGHT

    1 envelope plain gelatin
    ½ cup cold water
    1½ cups orange non-caloric carbonated beverage
    *Segments of 2 oranges

Sprinkle gelatin over cold water. Heat beverage and add gelatin; stir to dissolve it. Divide orange sections into 4 champagne glasses. Pour in gelatin mix. Add Candied Orange Peel. Makes 4 servings; each serving has ½ fruit.

CANDIED ORANGE PEEL

Remove membrane from orange peel. Cut peel into matchstick pieces. Cover with water. Bring to boil, discard water. Repeat once or twice to remove bitterness. Pour ½ cup orange non-caloric beverage into pan with orange peel. Cook until peel is soft and soda is absorbed. Cool. Sprinkle with granulated sugar substitute and use as topping for Orange Delight.

You may scallop edges of orange shell if you wish

Cut oranges in half. Scoop out orange and fill shells with cut-up orange and apples on a bed of lettuce.

Top with sprig of Watercress.

* *Limited food—see Menu Plan, p. 18-20, for legal amount.*

ORANGE SHELL

Serve cut up *oranges and *apples in a half orange shell from which fruit has been removed. The edges of the orange may be cut in a scalloped effect. Use ½ cupful of fruit in each shell, with a bed of water cress or cut-up lettuce leaves. The orange shell is unlimited, but count the fruit—½ cup equals 1 serving.

ORANGE SHERBET

I am going to tell you about sherbet—it's a beverage or frozen dessert made of fruit juice, sweetener and water, milk or egg white. Now you know, suppose you make up some of your own? There's no limit to the possibilities. Here's one good recipe.

    *1 glass skimmed milk
    *3 tablespoons concentrated orange juice
     ¼ to ½ teaspoon sugar substitute (to taste)

Combine ingredients. Stir well. Pour into freezer tray or into 2 custard cups. Place in freezer at coldest setting until frozen. Two servings—each counts as ½ fruit and ½ glass milk.

ORANGE GELATIN ICE

    1 tablespoon unflavored gelatin
    ¼ cup cold water
    1 cup hot water
    Grated rind of ¼ orange
   *¾ cup orange juice
    ½ teaspoon liquid sugar substitute
    2 tablespoons lemon juice

Sprinkle gelatin over cold water. Dissolve in hot water. Stir in grated rind. Add sugar substitute, orange and lemon juices. Srtain, cool and freeze in tray. Stir a few times while freezing. Serves 3. Each serving counts as ½ fruit.

ORANGE WATER ICE

*2 tablespoons concentrated orange juice
¾ cup water
¼ teaspoon sugar substitute

Combine ingredients. Freeze in refrigerator tray. When frozen, put into blender container and turn on high speed just long enough to break up ice. Serve at once. Tastes just like the water ice that Italian vendors used to sell in my childhood. Count as 1 fruit.

ORANGE ICE POPS

Pour *4 ounces orange juice into the plastic molds sold for this purpose; put the molds into freezer tray. Unmold and lick like ice pop. Half cup juice is one serving of fruit.

PEACH AND ORANGE SHERBET

*1 cup sieved, drained, canned peaches
6 packets (1½ teaspoons) granulated sugar
  substitute
*¼ cup unsweetened grapefruit juice
*¼ cup orange juice
1½ teaspoon lemon juice
*1 egg white, stiffly beaten

Turn temperature control of refrigerator to coldest setting. Mix peaches with granulated sugar substitute; add grapefruit, orange and lemon juices; mix well. Turn into freezing tray. Freeze until frozen 1 inch from edge of tray—about 20 minutes. Turn into a chilled bowl; with an egg beater, beat until smooth; fold in beaten egg white. Return to tray; freeze until just firm. (Don't forget to reset temperature control to normal.) Makes four ½-cup servings; each serving equals 1 fruit.

Note: You can use this dessert for luncheon only, with a main dish which includes egg yolks. One possible menu:

> *Hot Cabbage Soup for 4*
> *Egg Salad for 4:*
> Eight cooked egg yolks and 7 cooked egg whites mashed well and combined with finely diced celery. (The egg yolks and whites can be set in top of double boiler and cooked only until firm over hot water.) Mix with Sauce Chambord (see index for recipe). Serve on mixed greens and cucumber slices.
> *Toast*
> *Peach and Orange Sherbet*
> *Beverage*

PICKLED PEACHES

> 1½ cups water
> 1½ cups cider vinegar
> 1 tablespoon whole cloves
> 1 tablespoon whole allspice
> ½ teaspoon cinnamon
> 4 tablespoons sugar substitute (or to taste)
> *6 peaches, sliced

Combine water, cider vinegar, whole cloves, whole allspice and cinnamon. Boil 10 minutes, then add sugar substitute. Put in peaches and let cook gently until done. The same syrup may be used for other allowed fruit. One peach equals 1 fruit.

BAKED PEARS

Pare, halve and core *pears. Sprinkle with nutmeg and cinnamon. Put 1 tablespoon water or non-caloric ginger ale or soda in bottom of dish. Cover and cook about 1 hour. Small pears may be baked whole. Green coloring and crème de menthe flavor may be added when pears are cold.

BAKED PEARS AND PINEAPPLE

    *2 pears
     1 teaspoon sugar substitute
     1 teaspoon grated orange rind
    *¼ pineapple
     2 tablespoons lemon juice
     ¼ cup water or non-caloric ginger ale
     Powdered cloves

Pare, halve and core pears. Cut into slices. Sprinkle with sugar substitute and grated orange rind. Peel pineapple, remove core, slice thinly and put on pears. Sprinkle with lemon juice. Add water or non-caloric ginger ale. Dust with cloves. Bake 1 hour in 350°F. oven. Three fruits.

PARTY PINEAPPLE-LIME COOLER

    *7½ cups unsweetened pineapple juice
     1⅔ cups fresh lime juice
     1¼ cups lemon juice
     10 tablespoons liquid sugar substitute
     5 pints non-caloric ginger ale

Combine all ingredients except ginger ale; chill. Just before serving, add ginger ale. Pour over crushed ice or ice cubes in tall glasses. Garnish with lime slices. Makes 30 servings, one-half fruit each.

PINEAPPLE BASKET

Cut *pineapple lengthwise into quarters, leaving the leaves on each quarter. Using a sharp knife cut fruit from pineapple but leave a narrow handle of fruit across the top. Cut fruit into even pieces about 1 inch thick. Marinate them in non-caloric orange soda. Then place fruit back into pineapple shell, one piece slightly to left, next one slightly to right, etc., so they make a pretty pattern. Allowance: 1 quarter pineapple equals 1 fruit.

PINEAPPLE AND RHUBARB COMPOTE

Wash and peel rhubarb and cut into 1-inch cubes. Add an equal amount of fresh *pineapple, cut into cubes. Cover with non-caloric orange drink and add a few drops of liquid sugar substitute. Cook in oven, or slowly on top of stove, until pineapple and rhubarb are tender. Serve one cup as one serving of fruit.

STRAWBERRY AND RHUBARB MIX

> 1 envelope unflavored gelatin
> ¼ cup cold water
> 3 cups rhubarb cut into 1inch pieces
> 1 cup water
> 2 tablespoons liquid sugar substitute
> Few drops red food coloring
> ¼ cup carbonated non-caloric lemon soda
> *1 cup strawberries

Soften gelatin in ¼ cup cold water. Combine rhubarb and 1 cup water. Cover and cook until tender. Strain, press out all you can from rhubarb saving only the liquid. Add to softened gelatin, stirring to dissolve. Add sugar substitute and cool slightly. Stir in food coloring and lemon soda. Chill until mixture begins to thicken. Fold in berries and pour into wet ring mold. Chill until set. To serve, unmold on platter and fill center with greens.

STRAWBERRY ICE

   *1 quart fresh strawberries, puréed
   1½ cups water
   1½ tablespoons granulated sugar substitute
   2 tablespoons lemon juice

Combine all ingredients. Let stand about 10 minutes, stirring occasionally. Place mixture in shallow pan. Freeze about 1 hour or until mixture is frozen a half inch around edges. Place mixture in a bowl and beat with electric mixer until fluffy. Freeze another hour; beat again. Return strawberry ice to freezer. Freeze until firm. Makes 8 servings, 1 fruit each.

STRAWBERRY MOUSSE

   *2 cups strawberries
    Sugar substitute
   *1 pint Vanilla Ice Cream W.W. (see index for
      recipe)

Mash 2 cups strawberries and add liquid sugar substitute to taste. Fold into a pint of Vanilla Ice Cream W.W. and set in freezer for 2 hours. 4 servings, each counting as 1 fruit. Keep record of skim-milk intake.

STRAWBERRY SAUCE OVER STRAWBERRIES

   *4 cups hulled strawberries
    2 tablespoons water
    1½ tablespoons liquid sugar substitute

Crush 1 cup of the berries, add water and liquid sugar substitute. Pour over remaining whole berries and chill. Good with Ice Cream W.W. or on Orange Soufflé. Eight servings. One serving equals 1 fruit.

STRAWBERRIES IN THE SNOW

      3 envelopes unflavored gelatin
      ½ cup water
      4 cups boiling water
      2 tablespoons liquid sugar substitute
      2 tablespoons lemon juice
      Red food coloring
    *6 ounces cottage cheese, sieved or put through blender
    *2 cups sliced strawberries

Soften gelatin in cold water. Dissolve in boiling water. Add liquid sugar substitute, lemon juice, and a few drops of red food coloring. Add half of the gelatin mixture very slowly to the cheese, blending until smooth. Pour into a wet 5-cup mold; chill until set. Add strawberries to the remaining gelatin mixture. Pour strawberry mixture over cheese mixture; chill until set. To serve, unmold and garnish with additional berries, if desired.

STRAWBERRY DELIGHT

      1 envelope unflavored gelatin
      ¼ cup cold water
    *2 cups strawberries
      1 tablespoon liquid sugar substitute
      1 tablespoon lemon juice
      ⅛ teaspoon salt
      1 drop red food coloring
    *¼ cup nonfat dry milk
      ¼ cup ice water

Soften gelatin in cold water; dissolve over boiling water. Mash strawberries; add liquid sugar substitute, lemon juice, salt and coloring. Blend in softened gelatin; chill until mixture begins to thicken. Combine dry milk and ice water; beat on high speed of mixer until stiff; fold into gelatin. Spoon into a wet 1-quart mold. Chill.

You must use your daily allowance of milk. Skim milk or buttermilk may be used interchangeably and at any time of day, but do not exceed the alloted total. (If you use evaporated skim milk, reduce the daily allowance by half.)

WOMEN AND MEN: 16 ounces (2 cups) daily
TEENAGERS: 32 ounces (1 quart) daily

Be sure to count as part of your daily intake any milk added to coffee or tea, used in soup or dessert, or made into milk shakes or malteds.

265

BASIC MALTED

>   *1 glass skim milk
>   Sugar substitute to taste (¼ to ½ teaspoon)
>   3 ice cubes

Place all ingredients in blender container and purée for about 30 seconds or until frothy.

Note: I have had no trouble in using ice cubes in the blender, but most blender manufacturers recommend that the ice be crushed first to avoid damage to the blades. To crush ice wrap the cubes in a towel and hammer them with a mallet, small iron pan or similar heavy object.

BLACK CHERRY MALTED

>   *⅓ cup nonfat dry milk
>   ⅔ cup non-caloric black cherry soda
>   2-3 ice cubes

Blend in blender until frothy. Coffee, cola, or creme soda may be substituted if you prefer.

STRAWBERRY MALTED

>   *1 cup skim milk
>   *4 strawberries (sugar free)
>   ½ teaspoon liquid sugar substitute, or to taste
>   2 ice cubes

Blend in blender. No ice is needed when using frozen fruit straight from freezer.

ANOTHER MALTED VARIATION

Some Weight Watchers use *buttermilk to replace *skim milk.

PINEAPPLE MALTED

Add 2 tablespoons (or more) cut-up fresh *pineapple to Basic Malted and whip in blender. (One-quarter of a pineapple equals 1 fruit, so part of fruit will be left after you make malted.)

ORANGE MALTED

     *1 glass skimmed milk
     *1 peeled orange, cut up
      ¼ teaspoon sugar substitute
      Dash orange extract
      2-3 ice cubes

Blend in blender container. Very unusual.

EXTRACT MALTED

*⅓ cup nonfat dry milk
½ cup water
2 or 3 ice cubes
1 teaspoon sugar substitute, or to taste

Use ¼ teaspoon any desired extract or flavoring—vanilla, rum, mint, maple, black walnut, or brandy. Blend in blender until frothy.

COFFEE MALTED

*1 cup skimmed milk
½ to ¾ teaspoon powdered coffee
Sugar substitute to taste (¼ to ½ teaspoon)
3 ice cubes

Place all ingredients in blender for about 30 seconds or until mixture froths.

DOUBLE RICH MALTED

*⅔ cup nonfat dry milk
⅔ cup water
½ teaspoon sugar substitute
3 ice cubes
Any allowed flavoring (optional)

Put into blender container and whip to a froth. Count as two cups skim milk.

* *Limited food—see Menu Plan, p. 18-20, for legal amount.*

HOW TO MAKE YOUR OWN BUTTERMILK

Make *1 quart skim milk following package directions. Add *½ cup buttermilk and mix well. Let stand at room temperature until clabbered (a day or more), then stir gently to break up the clabber. Refrigerate and use as you would delicious buttermilk for that's what it is! To make thicker buttermilk add a heaping tablespoon dry milk.

BUTTERMILK SHAKE

*¼ cup frozen or fresh strawberries (unsweetened)
Liquid sugar substitute to taste
A little vanilla
*8-ounce glass buttermilk

Put in blender srawberries, liquid sugar substitute, vanilla and a little buttermilk. Add remainder after you have let blender run for few seconds. Then blend again. Can be made with any *fruit.

COFFEE MILK SHAKE FOR TWO

Put in mixing cup ⅔ cup *nonfat dry milk, 2 tablespoons instant coffee (Sanka if you like). Pour into tall mixing shaker with 2 8-ounce glasses of water, 1½ teaspoons liquid sugar substitute (more if needed). Shake well. Chill before serving.

ORANGE SHAKE

*1 cup orange juice
*¼ cup nonfat dry milk
1 envelope granulated sugar substitute
1 drop vanilla

Combine in a pint jar. Shake well and serve over ice for a refreshing and satisfying drink.

WHIPPED TOPPING #1

> *⅔ cup nonfat dry milk solids
> ⅔ cup water
> 4 teaspoons lemon juice
> 2 teaspoons *liquid* sugar substitute (granulated
>   sugar substitute makes this gritty)
> 2 teaspoons vanilla
> 1 teaspoon artificial butter flavor (optional)

Combine in mixing bowl and beat with electric mixer until this becomes the consistency of whipped cream. Use immediately or refrigerate and beat again before using. Lemon juice keeps this more stable than the Topping which follows. Makes 4 cups whipped topping; counts as 2 cups skim milk. (The usual serving of ½ cup must be counted as ½ cup skim milk.) Enjoy!

Note: In talking with members of Weight Watchers, Inc. I have been told of their many failures in attempting to make whipped topping. My conclusion is that they have given up too easily—this must be whipped for at least 10 minutes. It is not necessary to chill the ingredients or equipment, except perhaps in a very hot kitchen in the middle of summer.

WHIPPED TOPPING #2

> *⅓ cup nonfat dry milk solids
> ⅓ cup water

Beat together lightly in bowl. Place in freezer for 25 minutes. Take out and beat until like whipped cream. One serving. This one, because it is made without lemon, is less stable than the preceding Whipped Topping but some may prefer the unsweetened version. One-third cup solids equals 1 cup skim milk.

* *Limited food—see Menu Plan, p. 18-20, for legal amount.*

ICE CREAM SODA

A tall glass, a scoop of Vanilla Ice Cream W.W., a bottle of non-caloric carbonated soda (your choice), a couple of straws—enjoy!

MILK ICE

Recipe equals 1 fruit and 1 glass milk.

    1 teaspoon gelatin
  *1 cup skim milk
    2 tablespoons hot water
    ½ teaspoon vanilla
    Artificial sweetener to taste (about ¼ teaspoon)
  *8 strawberries (or whatever fruit you wish, or
        1 teaspoon instant coffee)

Soften gelatin in 2 tablespoons cold milk. Add 2 tablespoons hot water. Stir well to dissolve gelatin. Put all ingredients into blender. On low speed, blend until thick and creamy. Put into freezer for 15-20 minutes. Pour into chilled bowl and beat with electric or hand beater until creamy and free of lumps. Return to freezer until firm.

VANILLA ICE CREAM

    2 teaspoons unflavored gelatin
  *2 tablespoons cold skim milk
  *1 cup skim milk
    1 tablespoon liquid sugar substitute
    ⅛ teaspoon salt
    2 teaspoons vanilla
  *3 cups Whipped Topping

Sprinkle gelatin over 2 tablespoons cold milk to soften it. Heat 1 cup skim milk but do not let it boil, add sugar substitute and salt. Stir in the gelatin. Cool mixture, and add 1½ teaspoons vanilla. Refrigerate until thoroughly chilled.

Meanwhile make Whipped Topping: Combine 1 cup nonfat dry milk, 1 cup water and 1 tablespoon lemon juice. Whip with rotary beater, electric mixer, or blender until stiff.

Combine the two mixtures and put back in refrigerator tray to chill. Before the new mixture is frozen solid, stir it well, so that the gelatin does not settle at the bottom. Chill again and enjoy! Note: Other flavorings may be added with, or in place of, the vanilla—for example, peppermint extract, rum extract, strawberries puréed to make strawberry mousse, or strong coffee (about 1 tablespoon).

FROZEN COFFEE DESSERT

Prepare ½ cup Whipped Topping #1 for each serving. Then fold in some strong black coffee. Taste and add more if the mixture seems to need it, then pour into a tray and set into the freezer.

STRAWBERRY PARFAIT

Arrange in a parfait glass layers of *strawberries sweetened with sugar substitute and layers of Vanilla Ice Cream W.W. (see recipe above). Serve at once.

ICE CREAM SHERBET

    1 cup any flavor non-caloric carbonated beverage
    *⅓ cup nonfat dry milk

Beat thoroughly and put in freezer for approximately 1½-2 hours or until mixture becomes hardened but not frozen. Good for a hot summer day; like sherbet.

Happy Birthday to You!

WHOOSH

Your stomach doesn't know when it's your Birthday... sing a lot ... don't eat a lot !

EASY ICE CREAM

Freeze Whipped Topping #1 in refrigerator tray. Simple—good.

COFFEE WHIP

> 1 envelope unflavored gelatin
> ½ cup cold water (*skim milk may be substituted)
> 1½ cups hot strong coffee
> 1½ teaspoons liquid sugar substitute
> ½ teaspoon vanilla
> Dash of salt

Sprinkle gelatin on cold water to soften. Dissolve in hot coffee; add sugar substitute, vanilla, and salt; chill in mixing bowl until syrupy. Beat thickened gelatin with rotary beater until it almost doubles in volume; spoon into 6 sherbet glasses; chill until firm. Makes 6 servings. Serve plain or with Whipped Cream W. W. over which sprinkle instant coffee. Unlimited if water is used.

MAPLE BAVARIAN CREAM

    1 envelope unflavored gelatin
    2 cups water
    2 teaspoons instant coffee
    Sugar substitute to taste
    1 small capful maple flavor
 *1 teaspoon nonfat dry milk

Soften gelatin in ½ cup cold water. Bring 1½ cups water to boil. Add coffee, sugar substitute, maple flavor and gelatin mixture. Mix well and chill. When jelled put through blender with dry milk for 10-15 seconds. Refrigerate. This mixture will jell in about ½ hour in refrigerator after blending.

SPANISH CREAM SPONGE

 *2 eggs, separated
 *2 cups skim milk
  1 tablespoon unflavored gelatin
  4 teaspoons liquid sugar substitute
  Dash of salt
  ½ teaspoon vanilla

In top of double boiler, mix lightly egg yolks, skim milk, gelatin, sugar substitute, salt and vanilla. Cook over hot water for a few minutes until mixture coats the spoon, stirring constantly. Whip egg whites until stiff and fold into hot mixture. Pour into 6 custard cups and refrigerate until set. Count each serving as ⅓ egg and ⅓ cup milk.

   * *Limited food—see Menu Plan, p. 18-20, for legal amount.*

VITAL RECORDS

UNLIMITED FOODS

May be used freely at any time and in any desired amounts (subject of course to your having no physical condition which limits such use).

SEASONINGS

Bouillon cubes or envelopes
Soy sauce
Horseradish, red or white
Herbs, spices, mustard
Salt, pepper, paprika, garlic

Lemons
Limes
Vinegar, wine vinegar
Sugar substitute

RELISHES

Red Cabbage Relish
Dill Pickles

Spiced Rhubarb

LIQUIDS

Tea or coffee, hot or iced
   (without sugar, count
   milk used)

Non-caloric carbonated sodas
Club soda, seltzer
Water

UNLIMITED RECIPES
(See index for page numbers.)

DRINKS

Cola Libra
Lemonade
Rhubarb Punch

Sober Ox on the Rocks
Clear Consommé or Bouillon

SOUPS

Asparagus Bouillon
Asparagus Bisque in a Blender
Herbal Asparagus Soup

Bean-Sprout Soup
Cabbage Soup
Celery Soup

Chilled Chicken Consommé
and Cucumber Refresher
Escarole Soup
Black Mushroom Soup
Spinach Soup

Spinach Soup with Herbs
Mock Split-Pea Soup
(make without carrot
and onion)
Water-Cress Soup

SAUCES

Blender Basil Dressing
Celery Sauce
Cucumber Sauce
Chinese Sweet and Sour Sauce
Dill Marinade
Fines Herbes
Garlic Vinegar
Marinade for Lamb

Mint Sauce
Healthade Salad Dressing
Fresh Mushroom Sauce
Simple Parsley Sauce for Fish
Blender Lemon-Parsley Sauce
Pimento French Dressing
Basil Pimento Dressing
Spicy Salad Dressing

DESSERTS

Crystal Gelatin
Lemon Gelatin

Chilled Spiced Rhubarb
Stewed Rhubarb

SNACKS

"Roast Peanuts"
"Popcorn Bowl"

Rhubarb

SALADS (See Chapter 6)

RECIPES CONTAINING SMALL AMOUNTS OF LIMITED FOOD
(but these must be counted, see Food Record)

SAUCES

BBQ Baste
Cooked Barbecue Sauce
Garlic Tomato Juice Dressing
Italian-Style Gravy
Mustard Dressing
Pimento Sauce
Quick Tangy Dressing

Sea Food Cocktail Sauce
Tomato French Dressing
Tomato French Dressing
with Onion
Tomato Sauce
Thousand Island Dressing
Water-Cress Salad Dressing

SOUPS

Cream of Asparagus and
   Mushroom Soup
Curried Cream of Kale Soup
Cream of Spinach Soup W.W.

Creamed Soup
Vegetable Minestrone Soup
Quick Soup for One
Vegetable Soup

HELPFUL HINTS WHILE DIETING

1. DO NOT COUNT CALORIES. As mentioned previously, counting is a trap and 200 calories of cake is never a substitute for a 200-calorie lunch. You can't bargain with the diet.

2. WEIGH YOUR FOOD CAREFULLY. You'll be amazed at how much more will be on your plate when you weigh food rather than guess at its weight.

3. CARRY YOUR "BEFORE" PICTURE and a mental image of your ideal figure.

4. WEIGH YOURSELF ONCE A WEEK ONLY. Weight can fluctuate daily for various reasons. It is the weekly average weight loss that is important. Be sure to weigh yourself at the same time each week, on the same scale, under the same conditions. Record your weight on the Weekly Weight Record.

5. TAKE ADVANTAGE OF THE "FREE" FOODS allowed in this diet. Never allow yourself to be hungry.

6. BE AWARE THAT YOU ARE LEARNING NEW EATING HABITS even away from home. It is possible to follow this diet plan in any restaurant anywhere in the world, if you really want to.

7. DO NOT ALLOW sympathetic thin friends or envious fat ones to give you "permission" to deviate from your diet plan.

8. FOLLOW THE DIET HONESTLY. The key to successful weight loss and its maintenance is learning discipline and control.

9. THINK BEFORE YOU EAT. Tempted to gobble? Just stop and count to ten, look at your "before" picture, remember your reasons for wanting to reduce.

10. BE PATIENT!

YOUR GOAL

Charted below are the realistic weights which you should be able
to achieve by steady adherence to your Menu Plan.

WOMEN

HEIGHT	SMALL FRAME	MEDIUM FRAME	LARGE FRAME
4'9"	105	113	121
4'10"	107	115	123
4'11"	109	117	125
5'0"	112	120	128
5'1"	115	123	131
5'2"	119	127	135
5'3"	122	131	139
5'4"	126	135	143
5'5"	129	138	147
5'6"	133	141	151
5'7"	137	145	155
5'8"	141	149	159
5'9"	145	153	162
5'10"	149	157	165
5'11"	153	161	169
6'0"	157	165	173

MEN

5'0"	117	125	133
5'1"	120	128	136
5'2"	123	131	139
5'3"	126	134	142
5'4"	130	138	146
5'5"	133	141	149
5'6"	137	145	153
5'7"	141	149	157
5'8"	145	153	161
5'9"	149	157	165
5'10"	153	161	169
5'11"	157	165	175
6'0"	163	171	181
6'1"	169	177	187
6'2"	177	183	193
6'3"	183	189	199

TEENAGE GIRLS

HEIGHT	12 YRS.	13 YRS.	14 YRS.	15 YRS.	16 YRS.	17 YRS.	18 YRS.
4'2"	62						
4'3"	65						
4'4"	67						
4'5"	69	71					
4'6"	71	73					
4'7"	75	77	78				
4'8"	79	81	83				
4'9"	82	84	88	92			
4'10"	86	88	93	96	101		
4'11"	90	92	96	100	103	104	
5'0"	95	97	101	105	108	109	111
5'1"	100	101	105	108	112	113	116
5'2"	105	106	109	113	115	117	118
5'3"	110	110	112	116	117	119	120
5'4"	114	115	117	119	120	122	123
5'5"	118	120	121	122	123	125	126
5'6"		124	124	125	128	129	130
5'7"		128	130	131	133	133	135
5'8"		131	133	135	136	138	138
5'9"			135	137	138	140	142

TEENAGE BOYS

HEIGHT	12 YRS.	13 YRS.	14 YRS.	15 YRS.	16 YRS.	17 YRS.	18 YRS.
4'2"	58						
4'3"	61						
4'4"	64	64					
4'5"	68	68					
4'6"	71	71	72				
4'7"	74	74	74				
4'8"	77	78	78	80			
4'9"	81	82	83	83			
4'10"	85	85	86	87			
4'11"	89	89	90	90	90		
5'0"	92	93	94	95	96		
5'1"	96	97	99	100	103	106	
5'2"	101	102	103	104	107	111	116
5'3"	106	107	108	110	113	118	123
5'4"	109	111	113	115	117	121	126
5'5"	114	117	118	120	122	127	131
5'6"		119	122	125	128	132	136
5'7"		124	128	130	134	136	139
5'8"			134	134	137	141	143
5'9"			137	139	143	146	149

DAILY FOOD RECORD (Items to Be Counted)
(Use these pages or copy the columns into a notebook.)

DATE	FOOD	RECIPE PAGE #	FRUIT	EGG	CHEESE

FISH	MEAT	LIMITED VEGETABLES	MILK	TOMATO JUICE

WEEKLY WEIGHT RECORD

(To avoid marking book, you may prefer to record this in a notebook.)

I started the Weight Watchers Diet on _____.

My starting weight was _____.

DATE	WEIGHT	LOSS	COMMENTS THAT WILL HELP YOU NEXT WEEK

DON'T LET IT HAPPEN AGAIN!

You have now been shown the safe, the sane, the positive way to shed those extra pounds that have made you so unhappy. Consult the charts on the preceding pages and set your goal. You are filled with confidence and determination. We at Weight Watchers know the feeling well! Every one connected with Weight Watchers in any capacity has gone through the diet program. We are not mere theorists. We are active participants. You have our blessings and our good wishes.

Your personal success with the diet will become apparent in a very short time. You will see it in the descending reading of your scale. You will find it in your narrowing reflection in the mirror. If you are truly honest and faithful with yourself . . . then you can't help but be honest and faithful with the program. Then a new way of life . . . a new YOU will emerge. A YOU to be proud of.

At that point you will find the world has changed. The skies will be a little bit sunnier. The people a little friendlier. Your step a little gayer. You are filled with a sense of self satisfaction. Actually the world hasn't changed . . . but you have . . . physically and mentally for the better. And isn't that what you've wanted all along?

Also at that point you must take preventive steps. Don't ever let it happen again. You've made one tough journey along the road from overweight to normal weight. Don't make the mistake of having to travel it twice.

INDEX